Celebrate the Risen Christ

Celebrate the Risen Christ

Billy Graham

Franklin Graham

Jack Hayford

Anne Graham Lotz

Max Lucado

John MacArthur

Charles Stanley

Charles Swindoll

W PUBLISHING GROUP
www.wpublishinggroup.com
A Division of Thomas Nelson, Inc.
www.ThomasNelson.com

Published by W Publishing Group, a Division of Thomas Nelson, Inc.,
P.O. Box 141000, Nashville, Tennessee 37214.

Printed in the United States of America
03 04 05 06 07 5 4 3 2 1

Contents

Forward
vii

Charles Stanley
UNDERSTANDING THE FATHER
1

Billy Graham
WHY JESUS CAME
3

Franklin Graham
THE NAME
27

Max Lucado
A CINDERELLA STORY
33

Charles Stanley
THE GREAT SACRIFICE
41

Jack Hayford
AIM YOUR HARD QUESTIONS AT GOD, NOT MAN
43

John MacArthur
ALL CREATION GROANS
51

Jack Hayford
IT IS FINISHED
71

Charles Swindoll
A SUNDAY MORNING MIRACLE
79

Anne Graham Lotz
JESUS MAKES SINS FORGIVABLE...FOR EVERYONE
99

Franklin Graham
SEIZING HOPE
131

Acknowledgments
141

Dear Valued Guest,

For more than seventy years, Family Christian Stores® has been in the business of impacting lives for Christ. It is our highest calling to honor Christ in the way we do business. With this goal, we take extra care to offer a wide selection of Christian products designed to strengthen the hearts, minds and souls of believers and seekers from all ages and stages of life.

This book is an extension of our mission. We've selected inspiring messages from several of Christian publishing's most beloved authors–mainstays like Billy Graham, Max Lucado and Charles Swindoll– to encourage and challenge you as they examine the beauty and significance of Christ's resurrection. We've also provided valuable coupons so you can purchase the full books from which these chapters were selected.

Thank you for shopping Family Christian Stores and FamilyChristian.com. We appreciate your partnership in reaching families and communities with the gospel and grace of Jesus Christ. We ask that you pray for us as we seek to operate our company in a way that best fulfills the mission God has given us.

Answering the call to help strengthen
the hearts, minds & souls of our guests,

Dave Browne
President/CEO
Family Christian Stores

Understanding the Father

CHARLES STANLEY

God sent His Son, Jesus Christ, to earth to reestablish the personal line of communication that was severed by the Fall. Salvation is the first step we take toward knowing the intimate side of God's love.

Jesus came so we might understand the Father's undivided devotion toward us. Through His unconditional acceptance and grace, we find healing for our broken lives and hope for the future.

But some say, "If only you knew my past, you would know why Jesus would never love me." To thoughts like these, Jesus replies, "Come to me, all you who labor and are heavy laden [that is, burdened by sin, anxious thoughts, and feelings of fear], and I will give you rest. Take my yoke upon you and learn from Me, for I am gentle and lowly in heart, and you will find rest for your souls. For my yoke is easy and my burden is light" *(Matt. 11:28–30)*.

Christ's birth provided the freedom man longed to experience. Through His life and death, our past is made clean *(Isa. 1:18)*. Through His resurrection, we find strength and courage to try again. He is your intimate Friend, One who is never ashamed to gather you in His strong arms of love.

—Charles Stanley
A Gift of Love

Why Jesus Came

Billy Graham

THE SON OF MAN HAS COME TO SEEK AND TO SAVE
THAT WHICH WAS LOST. –LUKE 19:10

We have seen that the most terrible, the most devastating
fact in the universe is sin. The cause of all trouble, the root
of all sorrow, the dread of every man lies in this one small
word—sin. It has crippled the nature of man. It has destroyed
the inner harmony of man's life. It has robbed him of his
nobility. It has caused man to be caught in the devil's trap.

All mental disorders, all sicknesses, all perversions, all
destruction, all wars find their original root in sin. It causes
madness in the brain and poison in the heart. It is described
in the Bible as a fatal disease that demands a radical cure.
It is a tornado on the loose. It is a volcano gone wild. It is
a madman escaped from the asylum. It is a gangster on the
prowl. It is a roaring lion seeking its prey. It is a streak of
lightning heading toward the earth. It is quicksand sucking
man under. It is a deadly cancer eating its way into the
souls of men. It is a raging torrent that sweeps everything
before it. It is a cesspool of corruption contaminating every
area of life.

But, as someone has said, "Sin can keep you from the
Bible—or the Bible can keep you from sin."

For ages men were lost in spiritual darkness, blinded
by the disease of sin, made to grope—searching, questing,

seeking some way out. Man needed someone who could lead him out of the mental confusion and moral labyrinth, someone who could unlock the prison doors and redeem him from the devil's prison. Men with hungry hearts, thirsty minds, and broken spirits stood hopelessly with searching eyes and listening ears. Meanwhile the devil gloated over his mighty victory in the Garden of Eden.

From the primitive man in the jungle through the mighty civilizations of Egypt, Greece, and Rome, bewildered men were all asking the same question, "How can I get out? How can I be better? What can I do? Which way can I turn? How can I get rid of this terrible disease? How can I stop this onrushing torrent? How can I get out of the mess in which I find myself? If there is a way, how can I find it?"

THE BIBLE'S ANSWER

We have already seen how the Bible teaches that God was a God of love. He wanted to do something for man. He wanted to save man. He wanted to free man from the curse of sin. How could He do it? God was a just God. He was righteous and holy. He had warned man from the beginning that if he obeyed the devil and disobeyed God, he would die physically and spiritually. Man deliberately disobeyed God. Man had to die or God would have been a liar, for God could not break His word. His very nature would not allow Him to lie. His word had to be kept. Therefore, when man deliberately disobeyed Him, he was banished from the presence of God. He deliberately chose to go the devil's way.

There had to be some other way, for man was hopelessly involved and helplessly lost. Man's very nature was inverted. He opposed God. Many even denied that God existed, so blinded were they by the disease from which they suffered.

But even in the Garden of Eden, God gave a hint that He was going to do something about it. He warned the devil and promised man, "And I will put enmity between thee and the woman, and between thy seed and her seed; it shall bruise thy head, and thou shalt bruise his heel" *(Gen. 3:15)*. "And thou shalt bruise his heel"—here was a brilliant flash of light from heaven. The head refers to a total permanent wound; the heel refers to a temporary injury. Here was a promise. Here was something that man could hold on to. God was promising that someday a Redeemer would come, a Deliverer would come. God gave man hope. Down through the centuries man held on to that one bit of hope!

That was not all. There were other occasions through the thousands of years of history when other flashes of light came from heaven. All through the Old Testament, God gave man the promise of salvation if by faith he would believe in the coming Redeemer. Therefore God began to teach His people that man could only be saved by substitution. Someone else would have to pay the penalty for man's redemption.

Go Back to Eden

Go back again with me in your imagination to Eden for a moment. God said, "In the day that thou eatest thereof thou shalt surely die." Man did eat of it. He died.

Suppose that God had said, "Adam, you must have made a mistake; that was a slight error on your part. You are forgiven. Please don't do it again." God would have been a liar. He would not have been holy, neither would He have been just. He was forced by His very nature to keep His word. God's justice was at stake. Man had to die spiritually and physically. His iniquities had separated him from his God. Thus man had to suffer. He had to pay for his own sins. As we have seen, Adam was the federal head of the human race. When Adam sinned, we all sinned. "Wherefore, as by one man sin entered into the world, and death by sin; and so death passed upon all men, for that all have sinned" *(Rom. 5:12)*.

The burning question became "How can God be just and still justify the sinner?" It must be remembered that the word justify means the "clearance of the soul from guilt." Justification is far more than just forgiveness. Sin must be put away and made as though it had never been. Man must be restored so that there shall be no spot or blemish or stain. In other words, man must be taken back to the position he had before he fell from grace.

For centuries men in their blindness have been trying to get back to Eden—but they have never been able to reach their goal. They have tried many paths, but they have all failed. C. S. Lewis says that "All religions are either a preview or a perversion of Christianity."

Education is important, but education will not bring a man back to God. False religions are an opiate that attempt to keep men from present misery while promising future glory, but they will never bring man to the place of his goal. The United

Nations may be a practical necessity in a world of men at war, and we are thankful for every step that can be taken in the field of international relations to settle disputes without recourse to war; but if the United Nations could bring lasting peace, man could say to God, "We do not need You anymore. We have brought peace on earth and have organized humanity in righteousness." All of these schemes are patchwork remedies that a sick and dying world must use while waiting for the Great Physician. Back in history we know that the first attempt of united man ended with the confusion of tongues at the Tower of Babel. Men have failed on every other occasion when they have tried to work without God, and they will continue to be doomed to such failures.

The question remains "How can God be just—that is, true to Himself in nature and true to Himself in holiness—and yet justify the sinner?" Because each man had to bear his own sins, all mankind was excluded from helping, since each was contaminated with the same disease.

The only solution was for an innocent party to volunteer to die physically and spiritually as a substitution before God. This innocent party would have to take man's judgment, penalty, and death. But where was such an individual? Certainly there was none perfect on earth, for the Bible says, "All have sinned" *(Rom. 3:23)*. There was only one possibility. God's own Son was the only personality in the universe who had the capacity to bear in His own body the sins of the whole world. Certainly Gabriel or Michael the archangel might possibly have come and died for one, but only God's Son was infinite and thus able to die for all.

GOD IN THREE PERSONS

The Bible teaches that God is actually three Persons. This is a mystery that we will never be able to understand. The Bible does not teach that there are three Gods—but that there is one God. This one God, however, is expressed in three Persons. There is God the Father, God the Son, and God the Holy Spirit.

The Second Person of this Trinity is God's Son, Jesus Christ. He is coequal with God the Father. He was not *a* Son of God but *the* Son of God. He is the Eternal Son of God— the Second Person of the Holy Trinity, God manifested in the flesh, the living Savior.

The Bible teaches that Jesus Christ had no beginning. He was never created. The Bible teaches that the heavens were created by Him *(John 1:1–3)*. All the myriads of stars and flaming suns were created by Him. The earth was flung from His flaming fingertip. The birth of Jesus Christ that we celebrate at Christmastime was not His beginning. His origin is shrouded in that same mystery that baffles us when we inquire into the beginning of God. The Bible only tells us, "In the beginning was the Word, and the Word was with God, and the Word was God" *(John 1:1)*.

About Christ, the Bible teaches us, "Who is the image of the invisible God, the firstborn of every creature: For by him were all things created, that are in heaven, and that are in earth, visible and invisible, whether they be thrones, or dominions, or principalities, or powers: all things were created by him, and for him: And he is before all things, and by him all things consist" *(Col. 1:15–17)*.

That last phrase indicates that He holds all things together. In other words, the entire universe would smash into billions of atoms were it not for the cohesive power of Jesus Christ. The Bible again says, "And, thou, Lord, in the beginning has laid the foundation of the earth; and the heavens are the works of thine hands: They shall perish; but thou remainest; and they all shall wax old as doth a garment; And as a vesture shalt thou fold them up, and they shall be changed: but thou art the same, and thy years shall not fail" *(Heb. 1:10–12).*

Jesus Christ, the Redeemer

Again Jesus said of Himself, "I am Alpha and Omega, the beginning and the end." He, and He alone, had the power and capacity to bring man back to God. But would He? If He did, He would have to come to earth. He would have to take the form of a servant. He would have to be made in the likeness of men. He would have to humble Himself and become obedient unto death. He would have to grapple with sin. He would have to meet and overcome Satan, the enemy of man's souls. He would have to redeem sinners out of the slave market of sin. He would have to loose the bonds and set the prisoners free by paying a price—that price would be His own life. He would have to be despised and rejected of men, a man of sorrows and acquainted with grief. He would have to be smitten of God and separated from God. He would have to be wounded for the transgressions of men and bruised for their iniquities, His blood shed to atone for man's sin. He would have to reconcile God and man. He would be the great Mediator of history. He would have to be a substitute. He would have to die in the place of sinful man. All this would have to be done—voluntarily.

And that is exactly what happened! Looking down over the battlements of heaven He saw this planet swinging in space—doomed, damned, crushed, and bound for hell. He saw you and me struggling beneath our load of sin and bound in the chains and ropes of sin. He made His decision in the council halls of God. The angelic hosts bowed in humility and awe as heaven's Prince of Princes and Lord of Lords, who could speak worlds into space, got into His jeweled chariot, went through pearly gates and across the steep of the skies, and on a black Judean night, while the stars sang together and the escorting angels chanted His praises, stepped out of the chariot, threw off His robes, and became man!

It was as though I, while walking along a road, stepped on an anthill. I might look down and say to the ants, "I am terribly sorry that I've stepped on your anthill. I've disrupted your home. Everything is in confusion. I wish I could tell you that I care, that I did not mean to do it, that I would like to help you."

But you say, "That's absurd; that's impossible. Ants cannot understand your language!" That's just it! How wonderful it would be if I could only become an ant for a few moments and in their own language tell them of my concern for them!

That, in effect, is what Christ did. He came to reveal God to men. He it is who told us that God loves us and is interested in our lives. He it is who told us of the mercy and long-suffering and grace of God. He it is who promised life everlasting.

But more than that, Jesus Christ partook of flesh and blood in order that He might die *(Heb. 2:14)*. "He was manifested to take away our sins" *(1 John 3:5)*. The very purpose of Christ's coming into the world was that He might offer up His life as a sacrifice for the sins of men. He came to die. The shadow of His death hung like a pall over all of His thirty-three years.

The night Jesus was born Satan trembled. He sought to slay Him before He was born and tried to slay Him as soon as He was born. When the decree went forth from Herod ordering the slaughter of all the children, its one purpose was to make certain of the death of Jesus.

THE SINLESS SON

All the days of His life on earth He never once committed a sin. He is the only man who ever lived who was sinless. He could stand in front of men and ask, "Which of you convinceth me of sin?" *(John 8:46)*. He was hounded by the enemy day and night, but they never found any sin in Him. He was without spot or blemish.

Jesus lived a humble life. He made Himself of no reputation. He received no honor of men. He was born in a stable. He was reared in the insignificant village of Nazareth. He was a carpenter. He gathered around Him a humble group of fishermen as His followers. He walked among men as a man. He was one of the people. He humbled Himself as no other man has ever humbled himself.

Jesus taught with such authority that the people of His day said, "Never man spake like this man" *(John 7:46)*. Every word that He spoke was historically true. Every word that He spoke was scientifically true. Every word that He spoke was ethically true. There were no loopholes in the moral conceptions and statements of Jesus Christ. His ethical vision was wholly correct, correct in the age in which He lived and correct in every age that has followed it.

The words of this blessed Person were prophetically true. He prophesied many things that are even yet in the future. Lawyers tried to catch Him with test questions, but they could never confuse Him. His answers to His opponents were clear and clean-cut. There were no question marks about His statements, no deception in His meaning, no hesitancy in His words. He knew, and therefore spoke with quiet authority. He spoke with such simplicity that the common people heard Him gladly. Though His words were profound, they were plain. His words were weighty, yet they shone with a luster and simplicity of statement that staggered His enemies. He dealt with the great questions of the day in such a way that, from simple to sophisticated, man had no difficulty in understanding Him.

The Lord Jesus cured the sick, the lame, the halt, and the blind. He healed the leper and raised the dead. He cast out demons. He quieted the elements. He stilled storms. He brought peace, joy, and hope to the thousands to whom He ministered.

He showed no sign of fear. He was never in a hurry. He met with no accidents. He moved with perfect coordination and precision. He had supreme poise of bearing. He did not waver or worry about His work. Though He did not heal all the sick, raise all the dead, open the eyes of all the blind, or feed all the hungry, yet at the end of His life He could say, "I have finished the work thou gavest me to do."

He stood before Pilate and quietly said, "Thou couldst have no power at all against me, except it were given thee from above" *(John 19:11)*. He told the frightened people that angelic legions were at His command.

He approached His cross with dignity and calmness, with an assurance and a set purpose that fulfilled the prophecy written about Him eight hundred years earlier: "He is brought as a lamb to the slaughter, and as a sheep before her shearers is dumb, so he openeth not his mouth" *(Isa. 53:7)*.

Defeating the Devil

He moved supremely, gloriously, and with great anticipation toward the mission that He had come to accomplish. He had come to save sinful men. He had come to appease the wrath of God. He had come to defeat the devil forever. He had come to conquer hell and the grave. There was only one way that He could do it. There was only one course set before Him.

His death had been prophesied thousands of years before. First, as we have seen, in Eden's Garden; and then in sermon, story and prophecy the death of Christ was set forth in the ages past. Abraham foresaw His death as the lamb was slain. The children of Israel symbolized His death in the slaughtered lamb. Every time blood was shed on a Jewish altar it represented the Lamb of God who was someday to come and take away sin. David prophesied His death in detail in more than one prophetic psalm. Isaiah devoted whole chapters to predicting the details of His death.

Jesus Christ said that He had power to lay down His life when He said, "The good shepherd giveth his life for the sheep" *(John 10:11)*. He said again, "Even so must the Son of man be lifted up: That whosoever believeth in him should not perish" *(John 3:14–15)*. Jesus Christ had faced the possibility of the cross far back in eternity. During all the ages that preceded His birth, He knew that the day of His death was hastening on. When He was born of a virgin, He was born with the cross darkening His pathway. He had taken on a human body in order that He might die. From the cradle to the cross, His purpose was to die.

Someone has described how He suffered as no man has ever suffered: "The night watches in Gethsemane, lighted by the flaming torches, the kiss of the traitor, the arrest, the trial before the high priest, the hour of waiting, the palace of the Roman governor, the journey to the palace of Herod, the rough handling by Herod's brutal soldiers, the awesome scenes while Pilate tried to save Him as priests and people clamored for His blood, the scourging, the howling multitudes, the path from Jerusalem to Golgotha, the nails in His hands, the spike through His feet, the crown of thorns upon His brow, the sarcastic and mocking cries of the two thieves on either side, 'You have saved others; now save yourself.'"

Sometimes people have asked me why Christ died so quickly, in six hours, on the cross, while other victims agonized on the cross for two and three days—and longer. He was weak and exhausted when He came there. He had been scourged, He was physically depleted. But when Christ died, He died voluntarily. He chose the exact moment when He expired.

There He hung between heaven and earth. Having suffered unspeakably, He voiced neither complaint nor appeal but simply a statement by which He let us know in two words something of the terrible physical pain He suffered when he said, "I thirst."

Some unknown poet has put it this way:

> But more than pains wracked Him there
> Was the deep longing thirst divine
> That thirsted for the souls of men,
> Dear Lord—and one was mine!

SINNER OR SUBSTITUTE

God demands death, either for the sinner or a substitute. Christ was the substitute! Gabriel and ten legions of angels hovered on the rim of the universe, their swords unsheathed. One look from His blessed face and they would have swept the angry, shouting multitudes into hell. The spikes never held Him—it was the cords of love that bound tighter than any nails that men could mold. "But God commendeth his love toward us, in that, while we were yet sinners, Christ died for us" *(Rom. 5:8)*.

For you! For me! He bore our sins in His body upon the tree. As someone has said, "Behold Him on the Cross, bending His sacred head, and gathering into His heart in the awful isolation of separation from God the issue of the sin of the world, and see how out of that acceptance of the issue of sin He creates that which He does not require for Himself that He may distribute to those whose place He has taken." Standing overwhelmed in the presence of this suffering, feeling our own inability to understand or explain, and with a great sense of might and majesty overwhelming us, we hear the next words that pass His lips, "It is finished."

But the physical suffering of Jesus Christ was not the real suffering. Many men before Him had died. Others had hung on a cross longer than He did. Many men had become martyrs. The awful suffering of Jesus Christ was His spiritual death. He reached the final issue of sin, fathomed the deepest sorrow, when He cried, "My God, why hast thou forsaken me?" This cry was proof that Christ, becoming sin for us, had died physically, and with it He lost all sense of the Father's presence at that moment in time. Alone in the supreme hour of mankind's history Christ uttered these words! Light blazed forth to give us a glimpse of what He was enduring, but the light was so blinding, as G. Campbell Morgan says, "that no eye could bear to gaze." The words were uttered, as Dr. Morgan has so well expressed it, "that we men may know how much there is that may not be known."

He who knew no sin was made to be sin on our behalf that we might become the righteousness of God in Him *(Gal. 3:13; Mark 15:34; 2 Cor. 5:21)*. On the cross He was made sin. He was God-forsaken. Because He knew no sin there is a value beyond comprehension in the penalty He bore, a penalty that He did not need for Himself. If in bearing sin in His own body He created a value that He did not need for Himself, for whom was the value created?

How it was accomplished in the depth of the darkness man will never know. I know only one thing—He bore my sins in His body upon the tree. He hung where I should have hung. The pains of hell that were my portion were heaped on Him, and I am able to go to heaven and merit that which is not my own, but is His by every right. All the types, the offerings, the shadows, and the symbols of the Old Testament were now fulfilled. No longer do the priests have to enter once a year into the Holiest Place. The sacrifice was complete.

Now that the ground of redemption has been laid, all the guilty sinner has to do is believe on the Son, and he can have peace with God. "For God so loved the world, that he gave his only begotten Son, that whosoever believeth in him should not perish, but have everlasting life" *(John 3:16)*.

THREE THINGS IN THE CROSS

In the cross of Christ I see three things: First, a description of the depth of *man's sin*. Do not blame the people of that day for hanging Christ on the cross. You and I are just as guilty. It was not the people or the Roman soldiers who put

Him to the cross—it was your sins and my sins that made it necessary for Him to volunteer this death.

Second, in the cross I see the overwhelming *love of God*. If ever you should doubt the love of God, take a long, deep look at the cross, for in the cross you find the expression of God's love.

Third, in the cross is the only *way of salvation*. Jesus said, "I am the way, the truth and the life: no man cometh unto the Father but by me" *(John 14:6)*. There is no possibility of being saved from sin and hell except by identifying yourself with the Christ of the cross. If there had been any other way to save you, He would have found it. If reformation, or living a good moral and ethical life would have saved you, Jesus never would have died. A substitute had to take your place. Men do not like to talk about it. They do not like to hear about it because it injures their pride. It takes all self out.

Many people say, "Can I not be saved by living by the Golden Rule? Or following the precepts of Jesus? Or living the ethical life that Jesus taught?" Even if we could be saved by living the life that Jesus taught, we still would be sinners. We still would fail, because not one of us has ever lived the life that Jesus taught from the time we were born till the time we die. We have failed. We have transgressed. We have disobeyed. We have sinned. Therefore, what are we going to do about that sin? There is only one thing to do and that is to bring it to the cross and find forgiveness.

Years ago King Charles V was loaned a large sum of money by a merchant in Antwerp. The note came due, but the King was bankrupt and unable to pay. The merchant gave a great banquet for the King. When all the guests were seated and before the food was brought in, the merchant had a large platter placed on the table before him and a fire lighted on it. Then, taking the note out of his pocket, he held it in the flames until it was burned to ashes.

Just so, we have all been mortgaged to God. The debt was due, but we were unable to pay. Two thousand years ago God invited a morally corrupt world to the foot of the cross. There God held your sins and mine to the flames until every last vestige of our guilt was consumed.

The Bible says, "Without shedding of blood is no remission" *(Heb. 9:22)*. Many people have said to me, "How repulsive! You don't mean to tell us that you believe in a slaughterhouse religion!" Others have wondered, "I do not understand why God demands blood." Many people have wondered, "I cannot understand why Christ had to die for me." Today the idea of the shed blood of Christ is becoming old-fashioned and out of date in a lot of preaching. It is in the Bible. It is the very heart of Christianity. The distinctive feature of Christianity is blood atonement. Without it we cannot be saved. Blood is actually a symbol of the death of Christ.

Recently I was standing at the admissions desk at Mayo Clinic in Rochester, Minnesota. There, in a little box, were a number of folders entitled "A Gift of Blood" lettered in red forming a large drop of blood. My first reaction was that this must be a gospel tract, but on looking more closely I saw that it was a challenge to people to assist in the blood program. Blood could mean the difference between life and death for someone ill in the hospital. No one who has ever had to receive a blood transfusion will look upon that blood with anything but gratitude. Some might say that blood taken is somewhat revolting, but blood given is a blessing!

The fact remains that blood represents life, as Leviticus 17:11 says, "For the life of the flesh is in the blood and I have given it for you . . . to make atonement for your soul." So the blood sacrifice runs throughout the Old Testament— a foreshadowing or a symbol of Christ's perfect sacrifice.

FIVE THINGS BLOOD BRINGS

The Bible teaches that it first of all *redeems*. "Forasmuch as ye know that ye were not redeemed with corruptible things, as silver and gold, from your vain conversation received by tradition from your fathers; But with the precious blood of Christ, as of a lamb without blemish and without spot" *(1 Peter 1:18–19)*. Not only are we redeemed from the hands of the devil, but from the hands of the law handed down by God through Moses. Christ's death on the cross brings me out from under the law. The law condemned me, but Christ satisfied every claim. All the gold and silver and the precious stones of earth could never have bought me. What they could not do, the death of Christ did. Redemption means "buying back." We had been sold for nothing to the devil, but Christ redeemed us and brought us back.

Second, *it brings us nigh*. "But now in Christ Jesus ye who sometimes were far off are made nigh by the blood of Christ" *(Eph. 2:13)*. When we were "aliens from the commonwealth of Israel, and strangers from the covenants of promise, having no hope, and without God in the world," Jesus Christ brought us nigh unto God. "There is therefore now no condemnation [judgment] to them which are in Christ Jesus" *(Rom. 8:1)*. The redeemed sinner will never have to face the judgment of Almighty God. Christ has already taken his judgment.

Third, it *makes peace*. "And, having made peace through the blood of his cross, by him to reconcile all things unto himself; by him, I say, whether they be things in earth, or things in heaven" *(Col. 1:20)*. The world will never know peace until it finds it in the cross of Jesus Christ. You will never know the peace with God, peace of conscience, peace of mind, and peace of soul until you stand at the foot of the cross and identify yourself with Christ by faith. There is the secret of peace. This is peace with God.

Fourth, it *justifies*. "Much more then, being now justified by his blood, we shall be saved from wrath through him" *(Rom. 5:9)*. It changes men's standing before God. It is a change from guilt and condemnation to pardon and forgiveness. The forgiven sinner is not like the discharged prisoner who has served out his term and is discharged but with no further rights of citizenship. The repentant sinner, pardoned through the blood of Jesus Christ, regains his full citizenship. "Who shall lay any thing to the charge of God's elect? It is God that justifieth. Who is he that condemneth? It is Christ that died, yea rather, that is risen again, who is even at the right hand of God, who also maketh intercession for us" *(Rom. 8:33–34)*.

Fifth, it *cleanses*. "But if we walk in the light, as he is in the light, we have fellowship one with another, and the blood of Jesus Christ his Son cleanseth us from all sin" *(1 John 1:7)*. The key word in this verse is all. Not part of our sins, but all of them. Every lie you ever told, every mean, low-down dirty thing that you ever did, your hypocrisy, your lustful thoughts—all are cleansed by the death of Christ.

Just As I Am

The story has often been told that years ago, in London, there was a large gathering of noted people, and among the invited guests was a famous preacher of his day, Caesar Milan. A young lady played and sang charmingly and everyone was delighted. Very graciously, tactfully, and yet boldly the preacher went up to her after the music had ceased and said, "I thought as I listened to you tonight, how tremendously the cause of Christ would be benefited if your talents were dedicated to His cause. You know, young lady, you are as much a sinner in the sight of God as a drunkard in the ditch or a harlot on scarlet street. But I'm glad to tell you that the blood of Jesus Christ, His Son, can cleanse from all sin."

The young woman snapped out a rebuke for his presumption, to which he replied, "Lady, I mean no offense. I pray God's Spirit will convict you."

They all returned to their homes. The young woman retired but could not sleep. The face of the preacher appeared before her and his words rang through her mind. At two o'clock in the morning she sprang from her bed, took a pencil and paper, and with tears streaming down her face, Charlotte Elliott wrote her famous poem:

> Just as I am, without one plea,
> But that Thy blood was shed for me,
> And that Thou bidd'st me come to Thee,
> O Lamb of God, I come! I come!
>
> Just as I am, and waiting not
> To rid my soul of one dark blot,
> To Thee, whose blood can cleanse each spot,
> O Lamb of God, I come! I come!

But this is not the end. We do not leave Christ hanging on a cross with blood streaming down from His hands, His side, and His feet. He is taken down and laid carefully away in a tomb. A big stone is rolled against the entrance of the tomb. Soldiers are set to guard it. All day Saturday, His followers sit gloomily and sadly in the upper room. Two have already started toward Emmaus. Fear has gripped them all. Early on that first Easter morning, Mary, Mary Magdalene, and Salome make their way to the tomb to anoint the dead body. When they arrive, they are startled to find the tomb empty. As Alfred Edersheim, the Jewish scholar, writes, "There was no sign of haste, but all was orderly, leaving the impression of One Who had leisurely divested Himself of what no longer befitted Him." An angel is standing at the head of the tomb and asks, "Whom do you seek?" And they reply, "We seek Jesus of Nazareth." And then the angel gives the greatest, most glorious news that human ear has ever heard, "He is not here, He is risen."

THE FACT OF THE RESURRECTION

Upon that great fact hangs the entire plan of the redemptive program of God. Without the resurrection there could be no salvation. Christ predicted His resurrection many times. He said on one occasion, "For as Jonah was three days and three nights in the whale's belly; so shall the Son of man be three days and three nights in the heart of the earth" *(Matt. 12:40)*. As He predicted, He rose!

There are certain laws of evidence that hold in the establishment of any historic event. There must be documentation of the event in question made by reliable contemporary witnesses. There is more evidence that Jesus rose from the dead than there is that Julius Caesar ever lived or that Alexander the Great died at the age of thirty-three. It is strange that historians will accept thousands of facts for which they can produce only shreds of evidence. But in the face of the overwhelming evidence of the resurrection of Jesus Christ they cast a skeptical eye and hold intellectual doubts. The trouble with these people is that they do not want to believe. Their spiritual vision is so blinded and they are so completely prejudiced that they cannot accept the glorious fact of the resurrection of Christ on Bible testimony alone.

The resurrection meant, first, that Christ was undeniably God. He was what He claimed to be. Christ was Deity in the flesh.

Second, it meant that God had accepted His atoning work on the cross, which was necessary to our salvation. "Who was delivered for our offenses, and was raised again for our justification" *(Rom. 4:25)*.

Third, it assures mankind of a righteous judgment. "For as by one man's disobedience many were made sinners, so by the obedience of one shall many be made righteous" *(Rom. 5:19)*.

Fourth, it guarantees that our bodies also will be raised in the end. "But now is Christ risen from the dead, and become the firstfruits of them that slept" *(1 Cor. 15:20)*. The Scripture teaches that as Christians, our bodies may go to the grave but they are going to be raised on the great resurrection morning. Then will death be swallowed up in victory. As a result of the resurrection of Christ the sting of death is gone and Christ Himself holds the keys. He says, "I am he that liveth, and was dead; and, behold, I am alive forevermore, Amen; and have the keys of hell and death" *(Rev. 1:18)*. And Christ promises that "Because I live, ye shall live also."

And fifth, it means that death will ultimately be abolished. The power of death has been broken and death's fear has been removed. Now we can say with the Psalmist, "Yea, though I walk through the valley of the shadow of death, I will fear no evil: for thou art with me; Thy rod and thy staff they comfort me" *(Ps. 23:4)*.

Paul looked forward to death with great anticipation as a result of the resurrection of Christ. He said, "For to me to live is Christ, and to die is gain" *(Phil. 1:21)*. As Velma Barfield on Death Row in North Carolina said: "I love Him so much I can hardly wait to see Him."

Without the resurrection of Christ there could be no hope for the future. The Bible promises that someday we are going to stand face to face with the resurrected Christ, and we are going to have bodies like unto His own body.

Face to face with Christ my Savior,
Face to face, what will it be?
When with rapture I behold Him,
Jesus Christ who died for me?
Face to face I shall behold Him,
Far beyond the starry sky;
Face to face in all His glory
I shall see Him by and by. *–Carrie E. Breck*

—Billy Graham
Peace with God

The Name

Franklin Graham

One of the great challenges in my ministry has been the work we do in difficult places. Over the years, I have worked extensively throughout Lebanon, Egypt, Jordan, Syria, and even Iraq. This is an area of the world that I love.

In some areas of the Middle East today, life has not changed much from Bible times. I have personally seen people living in goat-hair tents. I have witnessed camel caravans traveling across the desert. Seeing this makes the Bible come alive, especially as I read about Abraham, who searched for the land that God promised. I have a great love for the Arab people and have many personal friends who have given their lives to serve them.

One of my longtime friends, Aileen Coleman, is a missionary nurse who has served the Arab people for decades in the Middle East with modern medical care all in the Name of Jesus Christ. Our ministry, Samaritan's Purse, has assisted her on a number of occasions. Aileen told me a true story concerning the Bedouin tribes who still roam that land today.

"Bedouin" is an Aramaic name for desert dwellers. These people, perhaps strange to us, are rich in tradition and custom, much of which is very closely aligned to biblical teachings. These nomads are descendants of Abraham and Sarah's Egyptian handmaid, Hagar, and are often to be found speaking about "our great father, Abraham." He, too, lived in goat-hair tents, as did Isaac and Jacob, and they would be very much at home today among these wanderers of the desert. This story took place in the southern part of the Hashemite Kingdom of Jordan near Wadi Rum, a bleak and barren desert area well-known to the Bedouin people.

The story illustrates so powerfully in human terms the many facets of strength, protection, love, redemption, and power found through the integrity a name holds.

Safe in a Tent

As two boys, Abdul and Mohammed, were climbing the rocky terrain one day, they wound up in a heated argument. Abdul struck and accidentally killed Mohammed. As with others of different races and cultures, the Middle Eastern temper has a very low boiling point. Most of the time they vent their volatile emotions with ear-splitting cursing, flailing of their arms, and often with the flashing of gold-capped teeth. This young man had lost control, and now his friend lay dead on the stony landscape, a victim of second-degree murder. Abdul experienced the ultimate horror. Looking down, Abdul's heart sickened as he saw the limp body of his friend.

"Mohammed!" Abdul screamed.

Mohammed lay strangely still, his neck twisted.

"Mohammed, Mohammed!" Abdul shrieked, but Mohammed did not answer. Abdul shook him, trying desperately to get a response from his best friend. The lifeless body lay twisted on the jagged rocks. Abdul began to sob, the tears stinging his weather-beaten cheeks.

Mohammed was dead.

In Bedouin society, "an eye for an eye, life for a life" still prevails. Knowing the inflexible custom of his people, this young man ran across the desert in terror until he spotted the sprawling tent of the tribal chief. The youth, gasping for air, raced to the shelter, grabbed hold of the tent peg, and screamed for mercy. When the sheik heard the boy's cry he came to the door. The young man confessed his guilt and asked for protection.

It is a Bedouin custom that if a fugitive grabs hold of a tent peg and pleads for protection from the owner of that tent, if the owner grants protection, he will lay down his life for the one on the run. It is a matter of honor and duty; the integrity of the owner's name is on the line.

The sheik looked at the frantic young man, his knuckles white from gripping the tent peg so tightly. The old sheik put his hand on one of the guy-ropes of his tent and swore by Allah. "Go inside," the sheik said to the boy with a wave. "I give you my protection."

The next day, young men who had witnessed the crime came running toward the tent, shouting, "There he is! There's the killer!"

But the old man said, "I have given my word."

Now the boy's life depended on this old Bedouin's integrity.

"Out of the way! Give us the boy!" they yelled.

The old Bedouin sheik stood his ground. His name was respected in the village. His word was good. If these men, intent on revenge, laid a hand on Abdul, they would have to kill the old man first.

"Stand aside, sheik," a man yelled. "Give us the boy!"

The old man stood strong. "No." his voice rang out as he slipped his hand around the knife hanging around his waist.

"You don't understand," the pursuers argued. "that boy is a murderer. He has taken the life of another."

"I've promised him my protection. I will honor my oath," the sheik replied.

"Do you know who he killed?" the men argued.

"It doesn't matter," the sheik replied.

One of the men blurted out, "He killed your son— your only son!"

The old man flinched as if a knife had pierced his heart. His eyes filled with tears. There was a long silence. The old man's knees weakened. His face tensed.

On the floor of the sheik's tent, Abdul closed his eyes and buried his face, awaiting retaliation. Surely this was the end.

After a few moments, the old man softly spoke, "I'm an old man; I'll never be able to have another son."

Abdul felt his heart race. I'm dead, he thought.

"I have given the boy my protection," the sheik continued, "and I will honor my oath."

"What?" The pursuers were stunned. "How can you honor your oath when he's the one responsible for your son's death?"

In a hushed voice the sheik said again, "I am an old man. I cannot bring my son back to life. Because this boy came to me in the right way, I will take him as my own son and raise him. He will live in my tent and will be my heir. All that I have will be his. He will bear my name."

* * *

When I heard Aileen tell this story chills rushed through me. This was a picture of what God has done for mankind through the death of the One who bears the Name.

Just as with Abdul, eternal life or death for each of us depends on our finding protection, refuge, and redemption through the shed blood of Jesus Christ. As the Bible says, "Whoever calls on the name of the Lord shall be saved."[1]

The Apostle John said, "But as many as received Him, to them He gave the right to become children of God, to those who believe in His name."[2]

Believing in the Name of God's only Son is the real issue.

—Franklin Graham
The Name

1. *Acts 2:21 NKJV.*

2. *John 1:12 NKJV.*

A Cinderella Story:
The God Who Gave His Beauty Away

Max Lucado

God between two thieves. Exactly the place he wants to be.

Three men on three crosses, a well-known scene. Even casual students of Christ are acquainted with the trio on Skull's Hill. We've pondered their sufferings and sketched their faces and analyzed their words.

But let's imagine this scene from another perspective. Rather than stand on ground level and look up, let's stand at the throne of God and look down. What does God see? What is the perspective of heaven? Does God see the timber and nails? Does God witness the torn flesh and spilt blood? Can heaven hear the mallet slam and the voices cry?

Certainly. But God sees much more. He sees his Son surrounded by sin and two thieves covered with sin. A shadow hangs over their spirits. The crowd cringes at the sight of the blood on their skin, but heaven laments over the darkness of their hearts. Earth pities the condition of their bodies. Heaven weeps over the condition of their souls.

I wonder if we can understand the impact our sin has in heaven. We get a clue in Revelation 3:16 when Jesus threatens to spit the lukewarm church out of his mouth. The verb literally means "to vomit." Their sin, excuse the phrase, made God want to puke. Their acts caused him, not just distaste, but disgust.

Haven't you felt the same? Haven't you witnessed the horror of a human act and wanted to throw up? On last night's news broadcast the story was told of a ten-year-old boy who'd been allegedly set afire by his father. The man had stuffed tissue down his son's T-shirt, covered the boy with lighter fluid, and set him a flame. Why? Because the boy had taken some of the father's food stamps.

Doesn't such a story disgust you? Make you angry? And if we, who are also sinners, have such a reaction, how much more should a holy God? After all, it is his law being broken. His children being abused. His word being ignored.

His holiness being insulted.

The question is not, "Couldn't God overlook sin?" The question instead is, "How in the world is forgiveness an option?" The question is not why God finds it difficult to forgive, but how he finds it possible to do so at all.[1]

From God's angle the tragedy of these men was not that they were about to die, but that they were dying with unresolved sin. They were leaving this earth hostile to God, defiant of his truth, and resistant to his call. "When people's thinking is controlled by the sinful self, they are against God" *(Rom. 8:7)*. Sin is not an unfortunate slip or a regrettable act; it is a posture of defiance against a holy God.

Such is what heaven sees.

The figure on the center cross, however, has no such shadow of sin. "When he lived on earth, he was tempted in every way that we are, but he did not sin" *(Heb. 4:15)*. Stainless. Selfless. Even on a sinner's cross Jesus' holiness illuminates heaven.

The first criminal reads the sign that announces Jesus as the king of the Jews. He hears Jesus pray for those who kill him. Something about the presence of the carpenter convinces him he's in the presence of a king.

The other crook has a different opinion. "Aren't you the Christ? Then save yourself and us" *(Luke 23:39)*. You'd think a man near death would use his energy for something other than slander. Not this one. The shadow over his heart is so thick, even in pain he mocks.

Suddenly someone tells him, "You should fear God!" It's the voice of the first criminal. "We are . . . getting what we deserve for what we did. But this man has done nothing wrong" *(Luke 23:41)*.

Finally someone is defending Jesus. Peter fled. The disciples hid. The Jews accused. Pilate washed his hands. Many could have spoken on behalf of Jesus, but none did. Until now. Kind words from the lips of a thief. He makes his request. "Jesus, remember me when you come into your kingdom" *(Luke 23:42)*.

The Savior turns his heavy head toward the prodigal child and promises, "I tell you the truth, today you will be with me in paradise" *(Luke 23:43)*.

To those at the foot of the cross, the dialogue was curious. But to those at the foot of the throne, the dialogue was outrageous. They couldn't imagine it. How could the thief come to paradise? How could a soul speckled by sin go to heaven? How could a sinner be saved? They were about to see.

Did an angel move, did a demon stir as they witnessed the answering of the prayer? The sins of the thief (and all us thieves!) leave him and go to Jesus. Tiny specks at first, then large flakes, and finally layers of filth. Every evil thought. Each vile deed. The thief's ravings. His cursings. His greed. His sin. All now covering Jesus Christ. What nauseates God now covers his son.

At the same instant, the purity of Jesus lifts and covers the dying thief. A sheet of radiance is wrapped around his soul. As the father robed the prodigal, so now Christ robes the thief. Not just with a clean coat but with Jesus himself! "Baptized into union with him, you have all put on Christ as a garment" *(Gal. 3:27 NEB)*.

The One with no sin becomes sin-filled. The one sin-filled becomes sinless.

It is eternity's most bizarre exchange. Paul explained it like this: "Christ took away the curse the law put on us. He changed places with us and put himself under that curse" *(Gal. 3:13)*.

When he sees sin, a just God must either inflict punishment or assume it. God chose the latter. On the cross "God was in Christ, making peace between the world and himself" *(2 Cor. 5:19)*.

I know John says that Jesus was carrying his own cross as he walked up the hill, but he wasn't. He was carrying ours. The only reason he carried the cross was for us thieves and crooks. "Christ had no sin, but God made him become sin so that in Christ we could become right with God" *(2 Cor. 5:21)*.

It wasn't his death he died; it was ours. It wasn't his sin he became; it was ours.

A beautiful illustration of this came my way, even as I was writing this chapter. In between the composition of the two paragraphs above, I received a call from a friend named Kenny. He and his family had just returned from Disney World. "I saw a sight I'll never forget," he said. "I want you to know about it."

He and his family were inside Cinderella's castle. It was packed with kids and parents. Suddenly all the children rushed to one side. Had it been a boat, the castle would have tipped over. Cinderella had entered.

Cinderella. The pristine princess. Kenny said she was perfectly typecast. A gorgeous young girl with each hair in place, flawless skin, and a beaming smile. She stood waist-deep in a garden of kids, each wanting to touch and be touched.

For some reason Kenny turned and looked toward the other side of the castle. It was now vacant except for a boy maybe seven or eight years old. His age was hard to determine because of the disfigurement of his body. Dwarfed in height, face deformed, he stood watching quietly and wistfully, holding the hand of an older brother.

Don't you know what he wanted? He wanted to be with the children. He longed to be in the middle of the kids reaching for Cinderella, calling her name. But can't you feel his fear, fear of yet another rejection? Fear of being taunted again, mocked again?

Don't you wish Cinderella would go to him? Guess what? She did!

She noticed the little boy. She immediately began walking in his direction. Politely but firmly inching through the crowd of children, she finally broke free. She walked quickly across the floor, knelt at eye level with the stunned little boy, and placed a kiss on his face.

"I thought you would appreciate the story," Kenny told me. I did. It reminded me of the one you and I have been studying. The names are different, but isn't the story almost the same? Rather than a princess of Disney, we've been considering the Prince of Peace. Rather than a boy in a castle, we've looked at a thief on a cross. In both cases a gift was given. In both cases love was shared. In both cases the lovely one performed a gesture beyond words.

But Jesus did more than Cinderella. Oh, so much more.

Cinderella gave only a kiss. When she stood to leave, she took her beauty with her. The boy was still deformed. What if Cinderella had done what Jesus did? What if she'd assumed his state? What if she had somehow given him her beauty and taken on his disfigurement?

That's what Jesus did.

"He took our suffering on him and felt our pain for us . . . He was wounded for the wrong we did; he was crushed for the evil we did. The punishment, which made us well, was given to him, and we are healed because of his wounds" (Isa. 53:4–5).

Make no mistake:

Jesus gave more than a kiss—he gave his beauty.
He paid more than a visit—he paid for our mistakes.
He took more than a minute—he took away our sin.

—Max Lucado
A Gentle Thunder

1. *John R. W. Stott,* The Cross of Christ *(Downers Grove, Ill.: InterVarsity Press, 1986), 88.*

The Great Sacrifice

CHARLES STANLEY

Some people find it hard to believe that God is in the physical elements of the world today. They regard him as being removed and distant from His creation. But this is far from the nature of God. He would never speak life into the universe only to abandon it.

His sole intent is to reveal His love for you. And while He desires your love in return, He is committed to not pressuring you into a relationship with Him. For love to be sincere, it must come from the heart.

Jesus told His disciples that the greatest commandment a man or woman could fulfill was to love the Lord God above everything else (Matt. 22:37). Just as God came to earth to seek a personal relationship with us, we must seek His love above everything else.

Doing this requires personal sacrifice. However, God sacrificed His love first for us by sending His Son to earth to die for our sins on Calvary's cross. He could have remained in heaven where He was worshiped and adored, but He came to us so that we would know that He is a God who cares.

You can know without a shadow of doubt that God loves you. Ask Him to reveal His personal love for you. No matter what you are facing, God is still committed to you through the power of His eternal love. When you call to Him with a heart of love, He always answers.

—Charles Stanley
A Gift of Love

Aim Your Hard Questions at God, Not Man

Jack Hayford

My God, My God, why have You forsaken Me? —Matt. 27:46

It is perhaps the most dramatic word spoken from Calvary. It trembles with emotional anguish, and nothing dramatizes it more passionately than the heart-piercing cry of God's Son, feeling a sense of abandonment at the darkest moment of this very bad day: "Why? Why? Why have You left Me now?"

The actual words Jesus cried out are quoted directly from Psalm 22, a song by then already a thousand years old—a lyric David prophesied before anyone could imagine God's Messiah would become the One to fulfill its agony. To glimpse a part of it, read with me:

> My God, My God, why have You forsaken Me?
> Why are You so far from helping Me,
> And from the words of My groaning?
> O My God, I cry in the daytime, but You do not hear;
> And in the night season, and am not silent . . .
> All those who see Me ridicule Me . . .
> [They say,] "He trusted in the Lord, let Him rescue Him;
> Let Him deliver Him, since He delights in Him!"
> But You are He who took Me out of the womb . . .
> I was cast upon You from birth . . .

Be not far from Me,
For trouble is near;
For there is none to help.
Many bulls have surrounded Me . . .
They gape at Me with their mouths,
Like a raging and roaring lion.
I am poured out like water,
And all My bones are out of joint;
My heart is like wax;
It has melted within Me.
My strength is dried up . . .
And My tongue clings to My jaws;
You have brought Me to the dust of death.
For dogs have surrounded Me;
The congregation of the wicked has enclosed Me.
They pierced My hands and My feet;
I can count all My bones.
They look and stare at Me . . .
But You, O Lord, do not be far from Me;
O My Strength, hasten to help Me! *(vv. 1–2; 7–19)*

That was the cry of the psalmist in the spirit of the privileged candor that God welcomes from those who worship Him. He welcomes tears in His presence, for He isn't their source, and He allows complaints, for He alone can meet the needs. The counsel contained in Psalm 142 invites us to call in dark hours: "I cry out to the Lord with my voice . . . I pour out my complaint before Him" *(vv. 1–2)*. Again, the message is clear: aim your hard questions at God. You may not get the answer right then, but you can count on two things: (1) your cry never will fall on deaf ears, and (2) time will always bring an answer in your best interests. Always.

To scrutinize all the implications of this wrenching lamentation from Jesus' lips seems beyond human comprehension. We might be able to imagine the breaking in His voice or the anguish of His heart, but who can fathom the mystery of the separation taking place or the depth of the pain it struck to the soul of God's Son? This outcry born of inner agony was not a performance for melodramatic effect. No! The second person of the triune Godhead was experiencing a breach in the fellowship He had known with the eternal Father from before all worlds. And the separation— the cause of the forsakenness tearing at Jesus' mind— occurred because Jesus ("Him who knew no sin") was being made sin for us "that we might become the righteousness of God in Him" *(2 Cor. 5:21)*.

This concept staggers the finest theological minds and boggles the imagination of any who thoughtfully weigh its reality. And though the Bible explains it in the words from 2 Corinthians, and though the psalmist prophesied it long before the Son became flesh to fulfill His saving mission on our behalf, I don't know that any human can grasp the deepest mystery of the moment, but I do know two things are clear.

First, as the Son of God, Jesus was suffering in Himself the divine fulfillment of the ancient lesson taught in the Old Testament image of the scapegoat—the sin-bearer creature that was cast out from the camp, carrying all the guilt of the people. In His death somehow Jesus was totally absorbing in Himself both the guilt and the penalty of all the sin of all the ages—a feat that can be explained only in that His qualifications as a sinless Savior provided space for all sin to be swallowed up in His person. Then in dying, He fully broke the power of sin to ever again rule anyone who puts his life within the redeeming circle of His resurrected life!

Second, as the Son of man, Jesus was wrestling with an inexplicably dark depression, transcending description and beyond survival except for the miraculous sustaining power of the Holy Spirit. That grace alone, Hebrews 9:14 tells us, enabled Him to complete the offering of Himself to God as sacrifice on our behalf. Yet notwithstanding His divinity and the divine strength accomplishing this eternal and cosmically encompassing feat, the Lamb of the Cross was fully human as well. And He was devastated by the vacuum void of the Father's presence—bitterly crying as He actually drank the cup He pleaded in Gethsemane to avoid.

This is the central moment of Calvary: it is the fourth of seven words. It is filled with questions, with darkness, with a sense of ultimate forsakenness—God forsaken! Even if we never experience the dimension of Jesus' depression, all of us have had moments when we have wondered, "Why, God?" And then we know we have a Savior who has been there and understands our despair, and we have His example pointing us in the right direction. When you're in the middle of a bad day—or worse, when you feel sure you've lost touch with heaven and are mystified in your loneliness— aim your hard questions at God, not man.

Why? Because in life's darkest hours, there are usually no human beings with adequate answers. Counselors may analyze; associates may sympathize; experienced friends may empathize. But finite minds and feeble flesh can never satisfy us with the Presence we seek, for we truly cry for God Himself, not answers. When "bad day blues" turn black with the unanswerable, and everything you thought you knew backfires, forget human philosophies or riddling theologies. Cry out to God. He doesn't mind our complaints, and although He may seem absent, He's never far away. Ask my friend Bill.

The deal had crashed. It involved a seven-digit, multi-million-dollar figure for his corporation. After months of careful planning on the human side, and after more than two years of prayerfully seeking God's will and wisdom on the divine side, Bill as CEO had led his company to the brink of a pivotal acquisition. The funding was in place, and the promise of a broad range of new possibilities was open before them. The stockholders had been advised of the impending purchase, and the press was watching expec-tantly because of the innovation manifest in the development. And best of all, Bill's soul was clear before God as he moved forward with the plan.

Though the acquisition would advance profits dramatically, Bill knew his own heart before God. He had laid it before his Lord again and again during many months. He and his wife, Marie, had prayed together with unity and humility, "Dear Father, we want nothing but Your will—for our company, exactly as for our marriage. You are the Center of our lives: not success, not wealth, not recognition. We seek Your direction and blessing on Your terms, Lord. And whatever distills of profit or advancement, we present to

You in its entirety, not as a bribe to secure Your blessing, but as a sacrifice to honor Your name."

Then somebody pulled the rug out from under everything. The whole world was disintegrating around him like a rocket exploding on a pad at Cape Canaveral, the gantry tipping wildly from its base, its framework shattered and falling apart.

The whole deal threatened to collapse, and worse, the other company that had entered the agreement in apparent good faith had violated the carefully constructed terms and had secretly conspired to make Bill look like the culprit. Compounding his frustration was the fact that the other company's CEO claimed to be a Christian, and he was in many respects viewed as a man of spiritual values as well as moral principle. Driven by his fears and trapped in a newly surfaced but self-imposed difficulty, the other leader had turned the tables in a self-protective way that trashed the business agreement and proposed Bill as the cause of the problem. Bill was being named as the source of the deal's ruin. Bill's wisdom as a leader was in question, and his integrity as a businessman was being thrown toward the scrap pile. There was an "out," however.

The dishonesty of the other company—the calculated conspiracy that was besmirching Bill's good name—could easily be challenged in court. Bill only had to register his case and go public with charges that would vindicate him, even though the deal would be lost. At that point the Holy Spirit met Bill in his dilemma: God's Word summoned him beyond human wisdom to trust beyond tragedy.

The doubts of his shareholders were hanging over him like an impending cloudburst, and his employees were perplexed by negative reports on their otherwise trusted leader. Tempted to bitterness, stabbed with pain, torn by confusion, Bill cried out to God, "I don't get it! You know my heart. You know how I've sought You at every point. Why is this happening to me, Lord? I don't care about the loss of a potential expansion. You know that! But why have You thrown me out to the dogs of injustice?"

He laid before God's throne his complaint over the devastation of having sought God for direction, having received clarity and peace to proceed, and then seeming to have been forsaken by the One he had sought foremost to please. It was not a rebel's act of defiance but a child's cry of bewilderment. He bent over in prayer, doubled up with the physical torture of a soul driven to the edge. And one day during that season of his pained outcry before God's throne, God's Word resounded in his soul: "Do not take your brother to court. Do not defend yourself. Let Me be your Defender instead" *(1 Cor. 6:1–7; Ps. 7:10; 59:16–17; 62:1–8).*

Remembering the Savior's words in Psalm 22—the source of Jesus' cry from the Cross, "My God, My God!"—Bill was helped to wrestle through to his decision. His choice: "The deal may die, and my reputation be buried, but I will not defend myself." All human counsel would argue otherwise, but Bill determined to make God his sole point of complaint, inquiry, and defense. The outcome of his decision is almost too successful to be believed where human doubt, fear, and anger over injustice usually recommend reprisal and retribution. After an extended season, when things looked as if they would never change, during which Bill daily faced the need for keeping his commitment of trust to leave his case with God, a full resolution was realized. The deal was resurrected. No parties were embarrassed. All inequity was rectified. And Bill never publicly revealed the details of the whole story—not even afterward.

There is a price to making God your point of reference when the hard questions raised in the middle of a bad day rack your mind and torture your soul. It's the price of listening to His answers and deciding whether or not to submit to His way rather than your own. The rock-solid truth remains, the evidence of God's Word provides the unchanging, timeless assurance again and again: Your cry never will fall on deaf ears, and there will always be an answer—in His time—and that answer will be in your best interests. Always.

—Jack Hayford
How to Live Through a Bad Day

All Creation Groans

John MacArthur

Scripture records a number of supernatural phenomena that occurred while Jesus hung on the cross. Those events constituted God's own supernatural commentary on the cross. They are further proof of the extraordinary importance of what was occurring that day just outside Jerusalem.

The routes to the city that day were jammed with pilgrims coming and going as they prepared to celebrate Passover. Few if any of them realized the vital truth that God's true Paschal Lamb was dying that very day to provide forgiveness for all the sins of all the saints of all time. It was the very focal point of redemptive history, and yet as far as Jerusalem was concerned on that day, relatively few were taking notice. And few who witnessed the murder of Jesus had any idea of what was really taking place.

But then suddenly all nature seemed to stop and pay attention.

The Sun Darkened

The first of the miraculous signs that accompanied Jesus' death was the darkening of the sky. Matthew writes, "Now from the sixth hour until the ninth hour there was darkness over all the land" *(Matt. 27:45)*. Matthew was counting hours in accord with the Jewish system, so the sixth hour would have been noon. At the moment the noon sun should have been brightest in the sky, a darkness fell over all the land, and remained for three hours.

This was probably not a total blackness, but rather a severe darkening of the normal daylight intensity of the sun. "Over all the land" is an expression that might refer to the land of Israel, or it could refer to the whole world. I'm inclined to think that the sun itself was dimmed, so that the darkness would have been universal, and not limited to the local area surrounding Jerusalem.

It could not have been an eclipse, because Passover always fell on a full moon, and a solar eclipse would be out of the question during the full moon. God is certainly able to dim the sun's light. During Moses' time, darkness fell on Egypt because the plague of locusts was so thick that the flying insects blocked the sunlight *(Ex. 10:14–15)*. In Joshua's time the opposite occurred, and the sun seemed to stand still over Israel for a whole twenty-four-hour period *(Josh. 10:12–14)*. In Hezekiah's day, the shadows turned backward ten degrees, as the earth's rotation seemed to reverse for about forty minutes *(2 Kings 20:9–11)*. The darkening of the sun is commonly mentioned in Scripture as an apocalyptic sign *(Isa. 50:3; Joel 2:31; Rev. 9:2)*. Amos wrote of the last days of the earth, "'And it shall come to pass in that day,' says the Lord God, 'that I will make the sun go down at noon, and I will darken the earth in broad daylight'" *(Amos 8:9)*.

According to some of the church fathers, the supernatural darkness that accompanied the crucifixion was noticed throughout the world at the time. Tertullian mentioned this event in his *Apologeticuma*—a defense of Christianity written to pagan skeptics: "At the moment of Christ's death, the light departed from the sun, and the land was darkened at noonday, which wonder is related in your own annals and is preserved in your archives to this day."

Throughout Scripture, darkness is connected with judgment, and supernatural darkness of this type signifies cataclysmic doom *(cf. Isa. 5:30; Joel 2:2; Amos 5:20; Zeph. 1:14–15)*. Various interpreters have explained this darkness several ways. Some have suggested God sent it as a veil to cover the sufferings and nakedness of His Son, as an act of mercy toward Christ. Others have suggested it signified His displeasure with those who put Christ to death. Scripture does not say why the darkness; it only reports it as a fact. The darkness clearly does seem to signify divine judgment, and coming as it did during the time when Christ's suffering was most intense, in the three hours before He cried out, "My God, My God, why have You forsaken Me?" *(Matt. 27:46)* it may well signify the Father's judgment falling on Christ as He bore in His person our guilt.

In any case, the darkness is certainly an appropriate reminder that the cross was a place of judgment, and in those awful hours of darkness, Christ was standing in our place as the wrath of God was being poured upon Him for our transgressions. And that may well be why the biblical narrative links the culmination of the darkness with Christ's outcry to the Father: "And about the ninth hour Jesus cried out with a loud voice, saying, 'Eli, Eli, lama sabachthani?' that is, 'My God, My God, why have You forsaken Me?'

Some of those who stood there, when they heard that, said, 'This Man is calling for Elijah!'" *(vv. 46–47).*

Eli is Hebrew for God. (Mark uses the Aramaic cognate, Eloi.) *Lama sabachthani* is Aramaic, meaning, "Why have You forsaken Me?" Since Aramaic was the common language of the region, it seems unlikely that all the spectators at the cross were truly ignorant about the meaning of His words. Thus their remark ("This Man is calling for Elijah!") was a deliberate misrepresentation of His words—another cruel and sadistic sneer at Christ.

Their behavior makes clear their mocking intent: "Immediately one of them ran and took a sponge, filled it with sour wine and put it on a reed, and offered it to Him to drink. The rest said, 'Let Him alone; let us see if Elijah will come to save Him'" *(vv. 47–49).* The one who ran to fetch the vinegar obviously did so for melodramatic effect, to complete his mockery by pretending to be generous and compassionate to Jesus, but really only seeking another means to taunt. Vinegar would have been a disappointing refreshment to someone in such a state of dehydration though it would have helped some.

In fact, shortly after this, when Christ did utter the words, "I thirst" *(John 19:28),* the vinegar was all He was offered. By then it was close at hand *(v. 29)* because of this individual's devilish taunt. But at this point, other bystanders forbade the prankster from giving Christ even mock assistance, saying, "Let Him alone; let us see if Elijah will come to save Him." Despite the ominous darkness, they were reveling in Christ's sufferings, and they did not want anyone to offer Him relief even if the assistance rendered was merely a fiendish insult.

Matthew indicates that the taunting continued to the very end. It was at some point in the midst of that continued taunting that Christ said, "I thirst," and was then given a sponge full of vinegar. Shortly afterward, "Jesus cried out again with a loud voice"–saying "Telelestai!" then audibly giving Himself to God–He "yielded up His spirit" *(Matt. 27:50)*.

THE VEIL TORN

At the moment of Christ's death, a series of remarkable miracles occurred. Matthew writes, "Then, behold, the veil of the temple was torn in two from top to bottom" *(v. 51)*.

The veil was a heavy curtain that blocked the entrance to the Holy of Holies in the Jerusalem temple, the place where the Ark of the Covenant was kept, symbolizing the sacred presence of God. Josephus described the veil as ornately decorated, made of blue woven fabric.

Only one person ever traversed the veil, and that was the high priest. He entered the Holy of Holies only once a year, on the Day of Atonement, with the blood of a sacrifice. The veil was of vital symbolic importance, signifying "that the way into the Holiest of All was not yet made manifest" *(Heb. 9:8)*. In other words, it was a constant reminder that sin renders humanity unfit for the presence of God. The fact that the sin offering was offered annually and countless other sacrifices repeated daily showed that sin could not truly and permanently be atoned for or erased by animal sacrifices. "For it is not possible that the blood of bulls and goats could take away sins" *(Heb. 10:4)*.

"But Christ came as High Priest of the good things to come, with the greater and more perfect tabernacle not made with hands, that is, not of this creation. Not with the blood of goats and calves, but with His own blood He entered the Most Holy Place once for all, having obtained eternal redemption" *(Heb. 9:11–12)*. The tearing of the curtain at the moment of Jesus' death dramatically symbolized that His sacrifice was a sufficient atonement for sins forever, and the way into the Holy of Holies was now open. In effect, the entire Levitical system of rituals, animal sacrifices even the priesthood itself were done away in the moment of His death. The redeemed now had free and direct access to the throne of grace without the need for priest or ritual *(cf. Heb. 4:16)*.

The tearing of the high curtain from top to bottom signified that it was God Himself who removed the barrier. He was in effect saying, "My Son has removed this veil and eliminated the need for it, through a single, perfect, once-for-all sacrifice that cleanses the redeemed from their sins forever. The way into My holy presence is now open to every believer and the access is free and unobstructed."

At the moment the tearing of the veil occurred, the temple was packed with worshippers who were there for the killing of their Passover lambs. By God's design, it was in the very hour that those thousands of lambs were being slain that the true Passover Lamb died. He was the real Lamb whom all the others merely symbolized. In fact, He perfectly fulfilled all the symbolism of the worship in the temple. From that day on, all the temple ceremonies lost their significance, because what they were meant to foreshadow had finally arrived. Within forty years, the temple itself would be completely destroyed when Titus sacked Jerusalem. But the true end of the Old Testament sacrificial system did not occur with the destruction of the temple in A.D. 70. It ended here at the moment of Jesus' death, when God sovereignly declared Christ's death a sufficient sacrifice for sins forever, by supernaturally splitting the temple veil from top to bottom and opening the way into His presence.

THE EARTH SHAKEN

Another miracle also occurred at the exact moment of Christ's death. "And the earth quaked, and the rocks were split" *(Matt. 27:51)*. An earthquake powerful enough to split rocks would be a significant tremor. (The crowd in the temple probably assumed the earthquake was the cause of the tearing of the veil.) Such a powerful quake would be a frightening experience for everyone in the region of Judea. Although earthquakes were a fairly common phenomenon, an earthquake with enough force to split rocks would have instantly brought the entire city of Jerusalem to a halt for several minutes.

Earthquakes in Scripture are often used like darkness to signify a graphic display of divine judgment. In particular, earthquakes signify God's wrath. When Moses met with God at Sinai to receive the tablets of the law, "the whole mountain quaked greatly" *(Ex. 19:18)*. David wrote, "Then the earth shook and trembled; the foundations of the hills also quaked and were shaken, because He was angry" *(Ps. 18:7)*.

"The earth shook; the heavens also dropped rain at the presence of God; Sinai itself was moved at the presence of God, the God of Israel" *(Ps. 68:8)*. The prophet Nahum wrote,

> The Lord is slow to anger and great in power,
> And will not at all acquit the wicked.
> The Lord has His way
> In the whirlwind and in the storm,
> And the clouds are the dust of His feet.
> He rebukes the sea and makes it dry,
> And dries up all the rivers.
> Bashan and Carmel wither,
> And the flower of Lebanon wilts.
> The mountains quake before Him,
> The hills melt,
> And the earth heaves at His presence,
> Yes, the world and all who dwell in it. *Nahum 1:3–5*

The Book of Revelation indicates that the final judgment of the earth will commence with a global earthquake more powerful than any ever experienced *(see Heb. 12:26–27; Rev. 6:14–15)*. So it is clear that a supernatural earthquake like this one could only signify the wrath of God. At the Cross, the wrath of God against sin was poured out on God's own Son. The accompanying earthquake, coming at the culminating moment of Christ's atoning work, was a kind of divine punctuation mark, perhaps signifying God's anger at the fact that sin had cost His Son so much.

The Dead Raised

At that very same moment when Christ died, yet another miracle occurred: "The graves were opened; and many bodies of the saints who had fallen asleep were raised; and coming out of the graves after His resurrection, they went into the holy city and appeared to many" *(Matt. 27:52–53)*.

Many of the tombs in and around Jerusalem to this day are hollow stone sepulchers, resting at ground level or just above. The earthquake was evidently powerful enough to split sepulchers like these. That was not the miracle; that might have occurred in any earthquake. The great miracle is that those who emerged from the broken sepulchers were raised from the dead.

Of all the Gospel writers, only Matthew mentions this event. Some have cited this as a reason to discount Matthew's veracity, suggesting that if such an event occurred, it would have certainly been noteworthy enough to catch the attention of all Jerusalem. But there's no reason to think this miracle was designed to capture people's attention. It seems to have been a remarkably quiet miracle, despite its spectacular nature.

Although "many . . . saints who had fallen asleep" were raised, not all were. These were select representatives of the multitude of saints buried in and around Jerusalem. The number raised is not specified, but the term "many" in this case could refer to as few as a dozen or even fewer. (That would still be "many," given the fact that what Matthew is describing is people who were released from stone sarcophagi and came alive!) Still, despite the spectacular nature of the miracle itself, this seems to have been a fairly low-key event.

Notice, in fact, that those who rose from the dead did not appear in Jerusalem until after Jesus' resurrection. (The proper phrasing and punctuation of the verse is probably best reflected in the NIV translation: "They came out of the tombs, and after Jesus' resurrection they went into the holy city and appeared to many people.") Where these resurrected saints were in the days after they were loosed from the grave and before they appeared in Jerusalem is not specified. But the fact that they waited until after Christ's resurrection to appear to anyone reminds us that He is the firstfruits of those risen from the dead *(1 Cor. 15:20)*.

These risen saints most likely came forth from the dead in glorified bodies already fit for heaven (rather than being restored to life in unglorified mortal bodies, as Lazarus had been). They "appeared to many" *(Matt. 27:53)*. Again, how many is not specified, but evidently there were enough eyewitnesses to verify the miracle. When Matthew wrote his Gospel, some of the eyewitnesses would have still been alive. Matthew doesn't say what became of the risen saints, but they undoubtedly ascended to glory not long after Jesus' resurrection.

Their appearance proved that Christ had conquered death, not merely for Himself, but for all the saints. One day "all who are in the graves will hear His voice and come forth" *(John 5:28–29, emphasis added)*. This miraculous event prefigured that final great resurrection.

THE CENTURION SAVED

But perhaps the most important miracle that occurred at the moment of Jesus' death was the conversion of the centurion charged with overseeing the crucifixion. As Christ's atoning work was brought to completion, its dramatic saving power was already at work in the lives of those who were physically closest to Him. Matthew 27:54 says, "So when the centurion and those with him, who were guarding Jesus, saw the earthquake and the things that had happened, they feared greatly, saying, 'Truly this was the Son of God!'"

A Roman centurion was the commander of a hundred-man division (or a "century") the basic building block of a Roman legion. There were about twenty-five legions in the entire Roman army worldwide. Each legion comprised six thousand men, divided into ten cohorts of six hundred men each. Each cohort had three maniples, and each maniple was divided into two centuries. Each century was commanded by a centurion. The centurions were usually career officers, hardened men of war.

Because this particular officer was with those guarding Jesus, it appears he is the very one who had been given charge of overseeing and carrying out the crucifixion of Christ and probably the crucifixions of the two thieves as well. He and his men were close eyewitnesses to everything that had happened since Jesus was taken to the Praetorium. They had personally kept Him under guard from that point on. (It is even possible that the centurion and some of the men with him were also the same soldiers who arrested Jesus the night before. If so, they had been eyewitnesses

from the very beginning of the entire ordeal.) They had seen
how Jesus held His silence while His enemies hurled accu-
sations at Him. These same soldiers had strapped him to a
post for the scourging, and watched while He suffered even
that horrific beating with quiet grace and majesty. They
themselves had mercilessly taunted Him, dressing Him in
a faded soldier's tunic, pretending it was a royal robe. They
had battered His head with a reed they gave Him as a mock
scepter. These very same soldiers had also woven a crown
of cruel thorns and mashed it into the skin of His scalp.
They had spat on Him and taunted Him and mistreated
Him in every conceivable fashion and they had seen Him
endure all those tortures without cursing or threatening
any of His tormentors.

In all likelihood, the soldiers heard with their own ears
when Pilate repeatedly declared Jesus' innocence. They
knew very well that He was guilty of no crime that made
Him a threat to Rome's interests. They must have been
utterly amazed from the very beginning about how different
He was from the typical criminal who was crucified. At first,
they probably were inclined to write Him off as a madman.
But by now they could see that He was not insane. He fit
no category they had ever seen in the hundreds of crucifixions they had probably superintended.

Until now, the uniqueness of Christ had made no
apparent impact whatsoever on these soldiers. They were
hardened men, and Jesus' passivity made no difference in
the way they treated Him. His obvious innocence had not
gained any sympathy from them. They had showed Him

no mercy. They were professional soldiers, trained to follow orders. And so they had dutifully nailed Jesus' hands and feet to the cross. They had set the cross upright and dropped it into the hole dug for it. They had cast lots for Jesus' garments. And then they had sat down to watch Him die.

But Christ's death was unlike any crucifixion they had ever witnessed. They heard Him pray for His killers. They saw the noble way He suffered. They heard when He cried out to His Father. They experienced three full hours of supernatural darkness. And when that darkness was followed by an earthquake at the very moment of Christ's death, the soldiers could no longer ignore the fact that Christ was indeed the Son of God.

Mark suggests that there was something about the way Jesus cried out that struck the centurion as supernatural—perhaps the powerful volume of His cry, coming from someone in such a weakened condition. Mark writes, "When the centurion, who stood opposite Him, saw that He cried out like this and breathed His last, he said, 'Truly this Man was the Son of God!'" *(Mark 15:39)*.

Matthew indicates that it was also the earthquake, coming at the exact moment of Jesus' final outcry, that finally convinced the centurion and his soldiers that Jesus was the Son of God: "When [they] saw the earthquake and the things that had happened, they feared greatly" *(Matt. 27:54)*. Notice that Matthew indicates all the soldiers had the same reaction. When the earthquake occurred they "feared greatly" using a Greek word combination that speaks of extreme alarm. It's exactly the same expression Matthew used to recount how the three disciples reacted on the Mount of Transfiguration when Christ's glory was unveiled *(17:6)*. This kind of fear was a typical reaction of people who suddenly realized the truth about who Jesus is *(cf. Mark 4:41; 5:33)*.

When the soldiers around the cross heard Jesus' exclamation, saw Him die, and then immediately felt the earthquake, it suddenly became all too clear to them that they had crucified the Son of God. They were stricken with terror. It wasn't merely the earthquake that they were afraid of. Rather they were terrified by the sudden realization that Jesus was innocent and not merely innocent, but He was also precisely who He claimed to be. They had killed the Son of God. The centurion remembered the indictment of the Sanhedrin ("He made Himself the Son of God" *John 19:7*), and having witnessed Jesus' death up close from beginning to end, he rendered his own verdict on the matter: "Truly this was the Son of God!"

The words were evidently a true expression of faith. Luke says, "He glorified God, saying, 'Certainly this was a righteous Man!'" *(Luke 23:47, emphasis added)*. So the centurion and his soldiers with him were evidently the very first converts to Christ after His crucifixion, coming to faith at precisely the moment He expired.

The Drama Ended

John records that as the hour grew late, the Sanhedrin wanted the bodies off the crosses, so that they would not remain there overnight and defile the Sabbath. "Therefore, because it was the Preparation Day, that the bodies should not remain on the cross on the Sabbath (for that Sabbath was a high day), the Jews asked Pilate that their legs might be broken, and that they might be taken away" *(John 19:31)*.

The Sabbath was a "high" Sabbath because it was the day after Passover, and therefore that particular Sabbath belonged to the Feast of Unleavened Bread. The Sanhedrin's pretentious reverence for the sacredness of the high Sabbath is ironic in light of how they were treating the Lord of the Sabbath Himself *(cf. Mark 2:28)*. But it reveals again how they were wholly concerned merely for the appearance, and not the reality, of things. Old Testament law *(Deut. 21:23)* strictly commanded that the body of anyone hanged on a tree be removed and buried out of sight, not left hanging all night. It is almost certain that most victims of Roman crucifixion were nonetheless left hanging on crosses for days. But this being Passover, it was an especially high Sabbath, so the Sanhedrin wanted the Jewish law observed. That is why they petitioned Pilate not to permit the bodies to remain on the crosses overnight. In order to keep their sanctimonious veneer intact, they now wanted Jesus to die, and die quickly . . .

The breaking of the legs would make it certain that death would occur almost immediately, because once the legs could no longer push up to support the body's weight, the diaphragm would be severely constricted, and air could not be expelled. The victim would die of asphyxiation within minutes. The cruel practice also guaranteed that the victim died with as much pain as possible.

Soldiers from Pilate therefore came to the crucifixion site with the express purpose of breaking the victims' legs. John writes,

> Then the soldiers came and broke the legs of the first and of the other who was crucified with Him. But when they came to Jesus and saw that He was already dead, they did not break His legs. But one of the soldiers pierced His side with a spear, and immediately blood and water came out. And he who has seen has testified, and his testimony is true; and he knows that he is telling the truth, so that you may believe. For these things were done that the Scripture should be fulfilled, "Not one of His bones shall be broken." *(19:32–36)*

The legs of both criminals were broken. Within minutes, the forgiven thief was in Paradise with the Lord, who had preceded him to glory.

But the soldiers, finding Jesus already dead, decided not to break His bones. Instead, they pierced His side with a spear, to verify that He was dead. The blood and water that flowed out showed that He was. The watery fluid was probably excess serum that had collected in the pericardium (the membrane that encloses the heart). The blood was an indicator that the spear pierced the heart or aorta as well as the pericardium. The fact that blood and water came out separately from the same wound seems to indicate that death had occurred some period of time before the wound was inflicted, so that Christ's blood even in the area of the heart had already begun the process of coagulation.

Mark 15:43–44 says that after Jesus' death, Joseph of Arimathea came to ask Pilate for the body of Jesus, and "Pilate marveled that He was already dead; and summoning the centurion, he asked him if He had been dead for some time." The relatively early hour at which Christ died surprised all those who were familiar with death by crucifixion. He died several hours before the typical crucifixion victim would have been expected to die. (Remember that crucifixion was designed to maximize the victim's pain while prolonging the process of dying.)

But Christ died at such an early hour in order to demonstrate what He had once told the Jewish leaders: "Therefore doth my Father love me, because I lay down my life, that I might take it again. No man taketh it from me, but I lay it down of myself. I have power to lay it down, and I have power to take it again. This commandment have I received of my Father" *(John 10:17–18, KJV)*. He was sovereign, even over the timing of His own death.

Even the soldiers' failure to break His legs was a further fulfillment of Old Testament prophecy: "He guards all his bones; not one of them is broken" *(Ps. 34:20)*. And thus from the beginning to the end of the crucifixion, Christ had remained sovereignly in charge. The Father's will had been fulfilled to the letter, and dozens of Old Testament prophecies were specifically fulfilled.

Christ was dead, but death had not conquered Him. On the first day of the week, He would burst forth triumphantly from the grave and show Himself alive to hundreds of eyewitnesses *(1 Cor. 15:5–8)*. He not only atoned for sin, but He demonstrated His Mastery over death in the process.

The resurrection of Christ was a divine stamp of approval on the atonement He purchased through His dying. Paul wrote that Jesus was "declared to be the Son of God with power according to the Spirit of holiness, by the resurrection from the dead" *(Rom. 1:4)*. The Resurrection therefore gave immediate, dramatic, and tangible proof of the efficacy of Christ's atoning death. The converse is true as well: It is the Cross, and what Jesus accomplished there, that gives the Resurrection its significance.

A thorough account of all the events and eyewitnesses surrounding Christ's resurrection would fill another entire volume, so it is not possible to examine the biblical narratives of the Resurrection here. (Perhaps one day, if the Lord permits, I will have the opportunity to publish such a volume.) But it's worth noting that the Resurrection is one of history's most carefully scrutinized and best-attested facts. The enemies of the gospel from the apostles' day until now have tried desperately to impeach the eyewitness testimony to Jesus' resurrection. They have not been able to do so, nor will they.

Still, it is vital to see that the early church's preaching focused as much on the death of Christ as on His resurrection. Paul wrote, "We preach Christ crucified" *(1 Cor. 1:23)*; "I determined not to know anything among you except Jesus Christ and Him crucified" *(2:2)*; and, "God forbid that I should boast except in the cross of our Lord Jesus Christ" *(Gal. 6:14)*.

Why did Paul place so much emphasis on the death of Christ, rather than always stressing the triumph of the Resurrection above even His death? Because, again, without the atoning work Christ did on the cross, His resurrection would be merely a wonder to stand back and admire. But it would have no personal ramifications for us. However, "if we died with Christ," that is, if He died in our place and in our stead then "we believe that we shall also live with Him" *(Rom. 6:8)*. Because of the death he died, suffering the penalty of sin on our behalf, we become partakers with Him in His resurrection as well. That is virtually the whole point of Romans 6.

So don't ever pass over the meaning of the death of Christ on your way to celebrate the Resurrection. It is the Cross that gives meaning to the resurrection life. Only insofar as we are united with Him in the likeness of His death, can we be certain of being raised with Him in the likeness of His resurrection *(cf. Rom. 6:5)*.

That is why "Jesus Christ and Him crucified" remains the very heart and soul of the gospel message. And in the words of the apostle Paul, every believer's deepest yearning should be this: "That I may know Him and the power of His resurrection, and the fellowship of His sufferings, being conformed to His death, if, by any means, I may attain to the resurrection from the dead" *(Phil. 3:10–11)*.

—John MacArthur
The Murder of Jesus

It Is Finished

JACK HAYFORD

Tetelesthai—It is finished!

The most significant single word in the Greek New Testament translates to the most triumphant declaration. It contains both a prophecy and a verdict. Jesus, the Son, prophesied the momentarily impending conclusion of His saving work, and even before the Cross's finale, He anticipated the Father's verdict and His ultimate intervention.

The atoning sacrifice of the Lamb was accomplishing eternal salvation.

The deliverance of mankind was as possible as Israel's deliverance was from Egypt more than a millennium before.

The dawn of world redemption had broken, and with it the chains of human slavery to sin, shame, and condemnation were being shattered.

Though they were the most climactic, those were not the final words spoken by the Savior from the Cross. He would shortly commend His spirit into the Father's hands. But He was already confident; His declaration of triumph was being registered. The grounds were now established at a dual dimension: welcoming fallen humans back into fellowship with the Father and driving back the powers of evil from their dark and damning rule over mankind.

The essence of the magnificence in these words is their finality as a statement of faith. The ultimatum they declared was absolute, even though the victory was not yet visible. "It is finished!" was the Son of God's invitation to join Him in the conviction that now—because of the Cross—there is nothing we struggle with that is without either a purpose or an end.

No struggle need ever again be pointless.

No suffering need ever again be unending.

The Master not only announced salvation's total accomplishment, but near the climax of His bad day, He summoned us to embrace this truth when we're agonizing through ours. He was teaching us to learn and live in this light:

First, we never face any assault of flesh, devil, circumstance, or personal weakness, but that God's hand is present, mighty, and available to work through it all and beyond it all. This doesn't mean God has planned every bad thing that happens to people. Evil things that are initiated by hell's hatefulness or by human sin, failure, and rebellion create their own problems. But beyond them all, God's ultimate deliverance is our promised inheritance.

Second, Jesus' words "It is finished!" are to lead us to understand that even before our personal ordeals are over, we are privileged to invite God's sovereign presence and power to invade our bad days, releasing His triumphant grace to achieve His purposes in the end. The most incredible proposition in the universe is that the Sovereign of all creation awaits the invitation of frail humans. But once invited, the Father's transcendent power is ready to intervene—introducing a wisdom and might greater than anything producing the worst of our bad days.

The Cross demonstrates this point. When you're living through a bad day, don't expect to be able to "read" the full dimensions of God's redemptive plan in the middle of your struggle, but never doubt the certainty that it is in process. His call, "It is finished!" is our call to hold firm in this assurance: His sovereign power will ultimately win the day.

Karl and Pamela's baby died. The ordeal had been in progress for months. A horrible tumorous intrusion was crowding into the tiny infant's cranium, and at daybreak that Sunday morning the phone rang at our house. I spoke brief words of sympathy to the family friend who had called, advising me that the baby had succumbed to death, and almost immediately I left for the hospital. Karl and Pam were a strong pair in our congregation; they were parents already to three children, and they had so anticipated baby Jason's recovery, which would maintain a "two boys and two girls" evenness in the family.

I had wept with them the day before, bowing in prayer and uttering the one phrase the Lord had put on my lips: "Sustain this little boy unto life, O Lord, unto life!" I could not pray anything else, and I didn't give any interpretation to what I did pray. I have heard wonderful reports of miracles, especially in cases involving children, where God's creative reconstructive interventions have turned apparently futile circumstances into triumphant ones. We have had a small share in experiencing some of those miracles in our church family, but I have never felt it my privilege or assignment to declare one in advance of its occurring. Still, I had passionately prayed, "Unto life! Unto life!" But on the morning after, I was on my way to comfort a couple in a situation where death seemed to have won.

I turned the corner out of the subdivision where we lived, and I was slowing down to stop at the intersection's flashing red signal. It was still early, there was no other traffic, and as I slowed, I noticed a small object in the roadway. As I drew up to the crosswalk (there were no cars behind to goad me on after my stop), I got out to see what it was because I felt strangely moved to do so. There is no way to explain either my prompting or the scene that I saw other than to attribute it to the living God, who works signs as well as wonders. A dead sparrow lay there in the street—its head completely removed! The instant I saw it, a Voice deep within me—unprompted by human reason—whispered a message with clarity and conciseness: *Not one of them falls to the ground apart from your Father's will . . . Do not fear therefore; you are of more value than many sparrows (Matt. 10:29, 31).*

Returning to the driver's seat, I resumed driving to the hospital, my eyes brimming with tears and my mind racing even while my spirit soared with a deep sense of heaven's purpose invading Karl and Pam's moment. Whatever anyone else might say, I knew I had seen a sign, for there was no explanation why the bird would be lying there headless unless some purpose of God had arranged it. If a cat had snatched the bird and taken its head, it would have consumed the whole body. If a car had run over the bird, the head would have been on the pavement. Whatever happened—and at a timing that coincided with my arrival at the intersection—a message was clearly spoken to me: This baby whose head was taken is gone, but Father God wants you to be reminded that the child is precious to Him and that he is of great value to the Father!

That I felt this so profoundly was one thing, but how to relate it to a bereaved couple was another. It seemed to me that notwithstanding anything within my conviction, it could strike them as painfully contrived. But my uncertainty was instantly removed when I walked into the hospital room where Karl, Pam, and the couple who called me were embracing one another—praising God and worshiping Him for His goodness! They were not religious fanatics who blithely philosophized tragedy with a happy smile and a trite quoting of something like, "Everything is okay if you believe it's true." They were people who had been caught in the grip of God's grace and who had been persuaded by the Holy Spirit's comforting presence that beyond the tragedy, God was at work doing something grand. They didn't blame God or a deficiency of faith in Him for the event. They weren't bantering theological catchphrases or philosophical opinions. They had been secured in the arms of the Father and assured by the steadying pulse beat of His heart: There is a purpose to unfold from Jason's short life, and there will be an end to your sorrow as well.

Greeted with their warm embraces, I listened to their description of God's gentle preparation of their hearts for the baby's passing, and I prayed with praise alongside them. Then sensing the presence of the Holy Spirit's having worked such a wonder in the two bereaved hearts, I ventured telling of my experience while driving to the hospital. The response was, by now, predictable. No one needed to strain to make room for the episode, as though his spirituality was being tested by the response. They were stirred: "Indeed, Pastor Jack, the Lord is emphasizing the point. He has not only worked redemptively here in removing the pain of death's sting from our hearts in this moment; He is confirming to us that there is a purpose in this, not just a tragedy."

"From Tragedy to Triumph" suddenly became the theme of the day. The moment was so visited by divine grace, I couldn't help risking a suggestion: "Karl . . . Pam, let me ask your permission on something. I don't want to do anything that would risk appearing to exploit the emotion of the moment, but may I ask: Would you feel offended if I shared the story of this ordeal, along with this morning's events, with the congregation?" I could hardly believe my own ears. It was 6:45, and the first service would begin in forty-five minutes. I had a message ready, but I felt God had another one for our church family that day. Karl and Pam agreed, and the rest, to adapt a phrase, "is all He wrote!"

God inscribed a holy memory into the life of an entire congregation that day. He answered the doubts of people who wonder about premature death. He neutralized the superstitions that cause people to feel obligated to say God "designs" this kind of human agony. He fit together a combination of biblical good sense with human understanding. The result was not only a swelling of praise to God for His triumphs amid apparent tragedies, but that morning, more than thirty-five people received Jesus Christ as their Savior! (Yes, I did tell the sparrow story, and yes, the Holy Spirit made it credible to all hearts present, not as a rationalization but as a gracious illuminating providence reminding us of God's very personal care for each of us.)

His personal care is the reason that the events of any of life's bad days are a potential staging ground for the wonder of His redemptive working and a time you may witness signs of His personal attentiveness and care. When you're living through a bad day, there's a reason to declare, "It is finished!" All His purposes are secured and will be fulfilled, and whatever the present suffering, there is an end.

WEEPING MAY ENDURE FOR A NIGHT,
BUT JOY COMES IN THE MORNING. (Ps. 30:5)

—Jack Hayford
How to Live Through a Bad Day

A Sunday Morning Miracle

Charles Swindoll

It happens every Friday evening, almost without fail, when
the sun resembles a giant orange and is starting to dip into
the blue ocean. Old Ed comes strolling along the beach to his
favorite pier. Clutched in his bony hand is a bucket of shrimp.

Ed walks out to the end of the pier, where it seems he
almost has the world to himself. The glow of the sun is a
golden bronze now. Everybody's gone, except for a few
joggers on the beach. Standing out on the end of the pier,
Ed is alone with his thoughts . . . and his bucket of shrimp.

Before long, however, he is no longer alone. Up in the
sky a thousand white dots come screeching and squawking,
winging their way toward that lanky frame standing there
on the end of the pier. Before long, dozens of seagulls have
enveloped him, their wings fluttering and flapping wildly.
Ed stands there tossing out shrimp to the hungry birds. As
he does, if you listen closely, you can hear him say with a
smile, "Thank you. Thank you."

In a few short minutes the bucket is empty. But Ed
doesn't leave. He stands there lost in thought, as though
transported to another time and place.

Invariably, one of the gulls lands on his sea-bleached,
weather-beaten hat–an old military hat he's been wearing for
years. When he finally turns around and begins to walk back

toward the beach, a few of the birds hop along the pier with him until he gets to the stairs, and then they, too, fly away. And old Ed quietly makes his way down to the end of the beach and on home.

If you were sitting there on the pier with your fishing line in the water, Ed might seem like "a funny old duck," as my dad used to say. Or "a guy that's a sandwich shy of a picnic," as my kids might say. To onlookers, he's just another old codger, lost in his own weird world, feeding the seagulls with a bucket full of shrimp.

To the onlooker, rituals can look either very strange or very empty. They can seem altogether unimportant . . . maybe even a lot of nonsense. Old folks often do strange things, at least in the eyes of Boomers and Busters. Most of them would probably write Old Ed off, down there in Florida. That's too bad. They'd do well to know him better.

His full name: Eddie Rickenbacker. He was a famous hero back in World War II. On one of his flying missions across the Pacific, he and his seven-member crew went down. Miraculously, all of the men survived, crawled out of their plane, and climbed into a life raft.

Captain Rickenbacker and his crew floated for days on the rough waters of the Pacific. They fought the sun. They fought sharks. Most of all, they fought hunger. By the eighth day their rations ran out. No food. No water. They were hundreds of miles from land and no one knew where they were. They needed a miracle.

That afternoon they had a simple devotional service and prayed for a miracle. Then they tried to nap. Eddie leaned back and pulled his military cap over his nose. Time dragged. All he could hear was the slap of the waves against the raft.

Suddenly, Eddie felt something land on top of his cap.

It was a seagull! Old Ed would later describe how he sat perfectly still, planning his next move. With a flash of his hand and a squawk from the gull, he managed to grab it and wring its neck. He tore the feathers off, and he and his starving crew made a meal—a very slight meal for eight men—of it. Then they used the intestines for bait. With it, they caught fish, which gave them food and more bait . . . and the cycle continued. With that simple survival technique, they were able to endure the rigors of the sea until they were found and rescued.

Eddie Rickenbacker lived many years beyond that ordeal, but he never forgot the sacrifice of that first lifesaving seagull. And he never stopped saying, "Thank you." That's why almost every Friday night he would walk out to the end of that pier with a bucket full of shrimp and a heart full of gratitude.[1]

ANALYZING EASTER

Eddie's weekly ritual reminds me of our yearly Easter Sunday celebration. We get up before dawn, dress in our Sunday best, and gather—sometimes outside on a cold, windswept hilltop—for a sunrise service. Think how weird that must look to many people. And then, in our fashionable new outfits, we fight the crowd for a seat at another church service. Often those onlookers are actually in the service, of course. Once a year, on Easter Sunday morning, we look out across the church and, with sincerity and prayer, we toss out terms like "reconciliation" and "redemption," "resurrection" and "forgiveness."

For some who have been celebrating Easter most of their lives, this message has long since lost its edge. They've heard the words over and over again, but tradition has dulled the impact. I never really understood what Easter was all about until I was in junior high school, and then, frankly, I didn't care. I'd heard the same words every Easter for fourteen years.

For those to whom the message is unfamiliar, the words really don't mean much. To them Easter is colored eggs and bunnies and Spring Break in Daytona or Palm Springs. Yet we who are "in the know" assume that everybody speaks our language.

So what in the world is Easter all about? If I were to distill the Easter message into one sentence, it would be this: Jesus came back to life after He died. I could even put that message into one word: "resurrection."

"Resurrection" comes from resurge or resurgence, in the sense of "coming back" or "renewing" or "rising up." In other words, Jesus Christ, who was once down, dead, laid aside, crucified, later stood up miraculously and bodily. He "resurged." He came back to life, never to die again.

Most religions, and the world is filled with them, are built on philosophies. The four major world religions, however, are built on personalities, and of those four, only Christianity claims that its founder is still alive, having been resurrected from the dead.

Judaism, the oldest of the four, teaches that its founder was Abraham, and that is true. But historians tell us—in fact, the biblical record states, and Jews agree—that Abraham is dead. Around 1900 B.C., he died at "a ripe old age" and was buried by his sons, Isaac and Ishmael *(Gen. 25)*. Abraham is still dead.

Buddhism was founded by Buddha himself. The most ancient reliable piece of literature I could find regarding Buddhism says this of his death: "When Buddha died it was with that utter passing away in which nothing whatever remains behind." That pretty well seals the deal. No disciple of Buddha can declare, "I've seen the founder. He's been raised from the dead. I've spoken with him. He has appeared." Why? Because he is dead. Buddha is still dead.

Islam is founded on Mohammed and his teachings. Professor Childers, who has written a classic work on the subject of Islam entitled *The Light of Asia and the Light of the World*, writes this: "There is no trace of this founder having existed after his death or appearing to his disciples. Mohammed was born about A.D. 571 and died in A.D. 632 at the age of 61, at Medina, where his tomb is annually visited by thousands of devout Mohammedans." Not one follower of Islam could declare with proof that he has seen the risen Mohammed. Why? Because Mohammed died. He is still dead.

Unlike the founders of those three major world religions, the founder of Christianity, Jesus Christ is alive . . . and is still alive. His tomb is empty. He is risen. He is risen indeed!

His life was the watershed of history. His death and resurrection are the cornerstone of Christianity.

Wilbur Smith says, "The central tenant of the church is Christ's resurrection."

Robertson Nicoll writes, "The empty tomb of Christ has been the cradle of the church."

Michael Green, in his book *Man Alive*, states, "Without faith in the resurrection there would be no Christianity at all. The Christian church would never have begun; the Jesus Movement would have fizzled like a damp squib with His execution. You see, Christianity stands or falls with the truth of the resurrection. Once disprove it, and you have disposed of Christianity."[2]

What Bethlehem was to Jesus of Nazareth, the empty tomb is to Christianity. It's the keystone, the capstone, and the foundation of our faith. If He were still dead, we would have no living Savior, no living message. We would have only a series of dogma. But He is risen indeed.

After the horror of that crucifixion afternoon, darkness must have descended upon the hearts of the disciples as it had descended around the cross at Golgotha. Darkness, disillusionment, and great sorrow. Even the thought of a dawn of new hope seemed an eternity away to those depressed and confused disciples.

Easter's First Dawn

Early Sunday morning, just as the sun was rising, three women made their way through the mist to the tomb where Jesus had been buried. They weren't on their way to a sunrise service. They weren't on their way to worship and sing songs of praise. They weren't excited about what the future held. Their world had dropped out from under them. En route, they were wondering how they would ever get the stone rolled away from the tomb so they could enhance embalming the body of their crucified Master by adding fresh spices.

> And when the Sabbath was over, Mary
> Magdalene, and Mary the mother of James,
> and Salome, bought spices, that they might
> come and anoint Him.
> And very early on the first day of the week,
> they came to the tomb when the sun had risen.
> And they were saying to one another, "Who will
> roll away the stone for us from the entrance of
> the tomb?" *(Mark 16:1–3)*

But they worried unnecessarily. When they arrived the stone was rolled back, and an angel was sitting on it. Their worry was replaced with wonder. Have you ever done that? You worried about something, only to find that the problem was already solved, and a solution even better than you could have imagined had occurred?

The Apostle John, writer of the fourth gospel, had sixty years to ponder what had happened that bright and glorious morning. He wrote his gospel late in the first century about events that had happened about A.D. 35; so he'd had a long time to think about Jesus' ministry and all the events surrounding it. In the process, the Holy Spirit led him to write what is known today as the Gospel of John. Because he was an eyewitness to many events, John wrote with additional authority.

I think of that often when I read the accounts of the resurrection of Christ. What must it have been like to actually be there? What if I had come to that garden tomb in the misty morning hours, burdened with sorrow and loss, only to find the huge stone pushed aside and the tomb empty? What would my reaction have been? How would I have assessed the situation had I been one of His disillusioned disciples?

Jesus' disciples and other followers did not yet understand the resurrection. Then, they have their first encounter with the risen Savior.

> But Mary was standing outside the tomb weeping;
> and so, as she wept, she stooped and looked into
> the tomb; and she beheld two angels in white sitting,
> one at the head, and one at the feet, where the body
> of Jesus had been lying. And they said to her,
> "Woman, why are you weeping?" She said to them,
> "Because they have taken away my Lord, and I do
> not know where they have laid Him."
> When she had said this, she turned around, and
> beheld Jesus standing there, and did not know
> that it was Jesus.
> Jesus said to her, "Woman, why are you weeping?
> Whom are you seeking?" Supposing Him to be the
> gardener, she said to Him, "Sir, if you have carried
> Him away, tell me where you have laid Him,
> and I will take Him away."
> *(John 20:11–15)*

Peter and John had hurried to the tomb after Mary had alerted them to the disappearance of Jesus' body, and they had seen the evidence of the displaced stone, the empty tomb, and the disturbed-but-empty grave clothes. Not fully understanding how such things could have happened, the disciples had returned to their homes. But the men left too soon. Mary stayed, and because she did, she saw something much better than the lifeless evidence in and around the empty tomb.

Unforgettable Dialogue

Mary was weeping, overwhelmed with sorrow and grief and the reality of the events of the past few days. Once again she stooped to look into the tomb. Could it really be empty? Not only was her beloved Master dead, but now someone had desecrated His tomb. They had even stolen His body!

But when she peered inside the dark cave this time, she saw something even more startling: two angels in white. One was perched at the head of the burial slab, and one was perched at the foot. We're not told whether or not she recognized them as angelic beings, but my guess is that she did. How could she not? Considering their location and their appearance, it would seem obvious that Mary realized they were more than mere men. However, their presence was not as alarming to her as the Master's absence.

"Woman, why are you weeping?" they asked.

"Because they have taken away my Lord, and I do not know where they have laid Him."

Isn't it astonishing that Mary responded so matter of factly to a question from angels in white sitting inside an empty tomb? She was not blown away. She simply answered their question. Apparently, she was so preoccupied with the emptiness of the tomb that their identity meant little at that moment.

As soon as she said this, she turned around and saw another man standing there. It was the resurrected Jesus, but she did not recognize Him. The record states that she thought He was the gardener *(v. 15)*.

He asked her the same question the angels had just asked: "Woman, why are you weeping?"

Why didn't she know who He was? First, it was dark. Second, she was deeply troubled, her eyes blinded with tears. Third, she had no expectation of ever looking into Jesus' face again. He was the last person she expected to see. Fourth, He did not call her by name; He called her "woman," as though He did not know her or what had recently happened. "Whom are you seeking?" It's not surprising she didn't know who He was.

And so, thinking Him to be the gardener, she continued, "Sir, if you are the one who has taken Him away, tell me where you have taken Him."

And then He called her by name.

> Jesus said to her, "Mary!" She turned and said
> to Him in Hebrew, "Rabboni!"
> (which means, Teacher). *(John 20:16)*

"Mary!" Jesus said. And that's all He had to say. She had heard Him call her name many times before. She knew that voice! And she immediately recognized Him. "Teacher!"

As you would expect, she embraced Him. She reached over and embraced Him. She clung to Him. Some translations suggest that she merely "touched" Him. But the original Greek term that John uses means "to cling to." That becomes clear when we read Jesus' reaction:

> Stop clinging to Me, for I have not yet ascended
> to the Father; but go to My brethren, and say to
> them, "I ascend to My Father and your Father,
> and My God and your God." *(John 20:17)*

That is the whole point of Jesus' response to her: "Stop clinging to Me." Why would He say that if Mary were just touching Him? "Stop clinging to Me, for I have not yet ascended to the Father."

In this exchange, it seems clear that Jesus was establishing a new relationship with His followers. He wasted no time instructing Mary to carry that message to the other disciples. He was establishing a spiritual relationship, a relationship not based on touch and sight but on faith.

"Go to my brethren," He told her. Not only was He establishing a new relationship by calling His disciples His "brothers," He was also implying that they were now new relatives.

Earlier He had said they were friends: "I no longer call you servants . . . instead, I have called you friends" *(15:15)*. Believers in Jesus become a part of Jesus' family with God as their father . . . Mary's new responsibility was to testify to His risen presence.[3]

He went on to say, "Tell them that I will ascend to My Father and your Father, My God and your God."

> Mary Magdalene came, announcing to the
> disciples, "I have seen the Lord," and that
> He had said these things to her. *(John 20:18)*

After the disciples left the tomb they could say, "I have seen the evidence." But after Mary left the tomb she could say, "I have seen the Lord Himself, and He has said these things to me."

Now you would expect that those men who heard Mary's testimony would have said, "Tell us where He is. We want to see Him." You would expect them to rush out the door to meet the Savior, wouldn't you?

But Mark tells us they didn't do that.

> She went and reported to those who had been
> with Him, while they were mourning and weeping.
> And when they heard that He was alive, and had
> been seen by her, they refused to believe it.
> *(Mark 16:10–11)*

How could they deny what she had seen and refuse to believe what she had said? Some chauvinist might say, "Because it came from the lips of an hysterical woman . . . you can't trust the words of a woman when she's excited." But that is simply not true.

> And after that, He appeared in a different
> form to two of them, while they were walking
> along on their way to the country. And they

> went away and reported it to the others,
> but they did not believe them either.
> *(Mark 16:12–13)*

They refused to believe any of these eyewitnesses because they had thrown up a wall of rejection around their hearts and minds. People can hear one piece of evidence after another, but if the heart is not prompted to faith, they will not believe, no matter how clear and convincing the evidence. The hammer of truth may strike blow after blow to that wall of rejection, trying to remove one stone after another, and yet the wall stands fast. Candidly, some of you who are reading this book are saying, "I've never believed it, never will, never plan to. Trot out as many eyewitnesses as you want: I just do not and will not believe it."

My answer to you? Well, maybe not yet. Someday, I'm praying, you will.

> And afterward He appeared to the eleven
> themselves as they were reclining at the table;
> and He reproached them for their unbelief
> and hardness of heart, because they had not
> believed those who had seen Him after He
> had risen. *(Mark 16:14)*

Finally Jesus Christ Himself stood in the presence of the eleven disciples and "reproached them for their unbelief and hardness of heart." Their unbelief was illogical and their hard hearts inexcusable. Eye-witnesses had come to tell them of the risen Christ, yet they had not believed.

INDISPUTABLE EVIDENCE

That brings us to one of the most remarkable proofs of the power of Christ's resurrection: the transformation of the disciples.

The church has had centuries to deal with the fact of His resurrection from the dead. But imagine what it must have been like for Jesus' disciples and followers, who had just seen His bruised and broken dead body taken from the cross and buried. Even though Jesus had said, "When I die, I will come back again; and because I live, you will live also," they didn't understand what He meant. So unbelievable was it, that, when the disciples first heard that Jesus was alive again, from eyewitnesses, they did not believe it. But when they finally did believe, they were transformed.

We have immortalized the disciples as men of incredible courage and remarkable understanding. But they were not always that way. When Jesus Christ breathed His last gasping breath on the cross, these men returned to their homes and their former lives, the fishermen returned to their nets, sorrowful and totally disillusioned. Before they were apprehensive, now they were scared, because each one of them could be identified with the Jewish insurrectionist who had just been crucified. They denied, they doubted, and they fled. And yet, by the middle of the Book of Acts—no more than thirty years later—these same disciples and their converts were described as "these that have turned the world upside down" *(Acts 17:6 KJV)*.

The beginning of their transformation can be traced to that Sunday-morning miracle of Jesus' resurrection. He had been changed to a "glorified state," and they were now changed in their outlook . . .

Imagine it. Just a few days before they had walked with Him and eaten with Him and slept beside Him and talked with Him. Then came that horrendous betrayal in the darkness of Gethsemane—that turning point, after which nothing was ever the same again. Death—the most horrible form of death— came between them and their beloved Master. All they had hoped for and planned were lost. Their dreams were dashed, leaving them frightened and filled with doubt, until . . .

In a flash, as though time and space have been suspended, He has come back, bringing all sorts of new dimensions to their attention, as the power of God is unleashed in His new body. It was unbelievable.

Personal Empowerment

This dramatic performance of God's power is a preview of coming attractions. "Because I live, you will live also," Jesus had told them. And now, from that empty tomb, God begins to announce, "All is forgiven! Wrath is removed! There is hope!" These men are about to be empowered by the resurrected Christ. "Despair no longer."

And since Mr. and Mrs. Average Citizen don't know what to do with that message, they misread it.

No one ever said it in more simple terms than John Stott in his excellent little book, *Basic Christianity*:

> It's no good giving me a play like Hamlet or
> King Lear, and telling me to write a play like

> that. Shakespeare could do it; I can't. And it
> is no good showing me a life like the life of
> Jesus and then telling me to live a life like that.
> Jesus could do it; I can't. But if the genius of
> Shakespeare could come and live in me,
> then I could write plays like that. And if
> the Spirit of Jesus could come and live in
> me, then I could live a life like that . . .
> To have Him as our example is not enough;
> we need Him as our Saviour.[4]

That's it! Christ came back from the dead so we might live as He lived and claim the triumph He has provided. He didn't die just to be studied and oohhed and aahhed over; He died and rose again to offer, through His blood and His life, new life-transforming power to live beyond the dregs of depravity's leftovers. And the first evidence we see of this is in the lives of Jesus' once frightened and disillusioned followers.

One of the most outstanding examples is Peter, a man who denied his Lord three times on the night He was being tried. Yet when the barriers of denial and remorse had finally been broken down in his own heart, when grace gave him his new standing in Christ, Peter became the first spokesman to declare the message of the resurrection to the world. Do you remember his words? Talk about empowered!

> Men of Israel, listen to these words: Jesus the
> Nazarene, a man attested to you by God with
> miracles and wonders and signs which God
> performed through Him in your midst, just
> as you yourselves know—this Man, delivered
> up by the predetermined plan and foreknowledge

of God, you nailed to a cross by the hands of
godless men and put Him to death.
And God raised Him up again, putting an end
to the agony of death, since it was impossible
for Him to be held in its power.
This Jesus God raised up again, to which
we are all witnesses.
Therefore let all the house of Israel know
for certain that God has made Him both Lord
and Christ—this Jesus whom you crucified.
(*Acts 2:22–24,32,36*)

Peter, one of the eyewitnesses to the empty tomb and the resurrected Christ, had been transformed from a brash young fisherman into an articulate, stalwart man of faith and a fiery evangelist for the Lord. His transformed life began as a result of one great event: his Lord's triumphant resurrection. That became the turning point for Peter's survival and later success.

WE ARE HIS WITNESSES

The resurrection of Christ is based on historical evidence—not on emotion, but on evidence.

I once knew a man who was studying law at Stanford University. Being an unbeliever, he determined to study the case for the resurrection of Christ as his dissertation topic. He was a brilliant man and a thorough scholar. He read shelf after shelf of books on the resurrection, studying all angles and aspects of the case. Then, in his own words, "Late one night I turned out the lights in my study, and I got down on my face beside my desk and said, 'Oh, God. I believe it.'" Why? Because he was an honest, intelligent searcher who could no longer deny the facts. The weight of the evidence finally crushed his stubborn will, and he surrendered in faith.

"No weapon has ever been forged, and none ever will be, to destroy rational confidence in the historical records of this epochal and predicted event," writes Wilbur Smith. "The resurrection of Christ is the very citadel of the Christian faith. This is the doctrine that turned the world upside down in the first century and that lifted Christianity preeminently above Judaism and all the pagan religions of the Mediterranean world."[5]

The tomb of Abraham is occupied. The tomb of Buddha is occupied. The tomb of Mohammed is occupied. But the tomb of Jesus Christ is empty.

Christianity alone is based on a living Person—the resurrected Son of God. And this resurrected Christ offers sufficient power to transform our lives.

As a result, like Old Ed used to do on the end of that pier every Friday evening, we spend the rest of our lives saying, "Thank You. Thank You."

—Charles Swindoll
The Darkness and the Dawn

1. *Max Lucado,* In the Eye of the Storm *(Nashville, Tenn.: Word Publishing, 1991), pp. 221, 225-226.*

2. *Michael Green,* Man Alive *(Downers Grove, Ill.: InterVarsity Press, 1968), n. p.*

3. *John F. Walvoord, Roy B. Zuck, eds.,* The Bible Knowledge Commentary, *(Colorado Springs, Colo.: Victor Books, 1983), Vol. 2, p. 343.*

4. *John R. W. Stott,* Basic Christianity *(Downers Grove, Ill.: InterVarsity Press, 1958), p. 102.*

5. *Wilbur M. Smith, "Scientists and the Resurrection," in* Christianity Today, *April 15, 1957.*

Jesus Makes Sin Forgivable...
For Everyone

Anne Graham Lotz

In the Old Testament, when a person sinned, he was required to take the very best, blue-ribbon lamb he could find, one without any spots or blemishes, to the priest at the temple. There, in front of the priest, the sinner would grasp the lamb with both hands and confess his sin. His guilt was transferred to the lamb as though it had traveled through his arms and hands to the terrified little creature. The priest would then hand the sinner a knife, and the sinner would kill the lamb so that it was obvious the lamb had died as a result of the sinner's action. Then the priest would take the blood of the lamb and sprinkle it on the altar to make atonement for the man's sin.

Throughout the years, fountains of blood and rivers of blood and oceans of blood flowed from the temple altar as God's children sought His forgiveness for their sin. Yet when they walked away from such a sacrifice, their hearts must have remained heavy as the burden of guilt clung like river slime to their souls. The writer to the Hebrews put it bluntly: "It is impossible for the blood of bulls and goats [and lambs] to take away sins."[1] So why the sacrificial slaughter?

The entire bloody ritual was like an IOU note that bought the sinner temporary atonement until a perfect sacrifice would come and pay it off. And the perfect Sacrifice did come.

One day, as John the Baptist was standing beside the River Jordan, a rather ordinary-looking man walked past. John recognized Him as his cousin, Jesus of Nazareth. But John didn't call Him by His given name. Instead, John pointed and identified Him as "the Lamb of God, who takes away the sin of the world!"[2] John was making the most remarkable announcement since the angels had heralded the birth of the Baby in Bethlehem. With razorlike perception, he recognized that Jesus Himself would be the perfect Lamb Who would pay off all those IOU notes with the sacrifice of Himself.

The pervasive misconception today is that since Jesus died as a sacrifice for the sins of the world, then we are all automatically forgiven. But we overlook the vital truth that we must grasp the Lamb with our hands of faith and confess our sins. We then must acknowledge that He was slain for our sins as surely as if we had plunged the knife into His heart. At that moment, the Lamb becomes our High Priest and offers His own blood on the altar of the Cross on our behalf. And, wonder of wonders! God accepts the sacrifice and we are forgiven! Our guilt is atoned for! We are made right in God's sight! Jesus, the Lamb of God, makes sin forgivable for everyone![3]

The Lamb Was Sacrificed

Following His six trials, Jesus was turned over to the Roman soldiers, who led Him to the place called Calvary for crucifixion.[4] Jesus had been on His feet for nine hours during which time He had been manhandled, spit upon, slapped, flogged, and dragged from place to place. His back was already a mangled, bloody mess from the scourging when the soldiers roughly placed a Cross on it, demanding that He carry His own means of execution through the streets of Jerusalem.

Onlookers and bystanders and curiosity seekers pressed in around Jesus as He dragged the heavy Cross through the cobbled, narrow city streets. Finally, His strength must have given way, causing His knees to grow weak and sending Him sprawling to the ground. It became apparent that He could not physically carry the Cross the distance to Calvary. So the soldiers, who surrounded Him like a human barricade, quickly solved the problem by seizing an unsuspecting gawker to carry the Cross for Him.[5]

At that precise moment, a man named Simon stepped out of obscurity and into the pages of history and the hearts of God's children. Not much is known about him except that apparently he came from Cyrene, implying that he was an African and therefore black. He must have had a powerfully built physique for the Romans to have spotted him so quickly and commanded his assistance.

Imagine what it would have been like to be Simon, and to have carried the Cross of Christ while following Him up Calvary.

What would it have been like to have endured the jeers and the cheers that swirled around Him like a golfer's gallery in hell?

What would it have been like to have shared in the humiliation of rejection as He was cast out of the city as though He wasn't good enough to remain inside?

What would it have been like to have felt the sticky warmth of His blood from the Cross on your skin?

What would it have been like to have felt the encroaching horror as the place of execution neared?

What would it have been like to have looked up through the sweat that trickled down your face, and see the executioners who stood waiting impassively with hammers in hand?

What would it have been like to have the burden of the Cross lifted from your back as someone said, "This is His Cross; you're free to go now," and He was nailed to it, not you?

Did Jesus catch Simon's eye and whisper a hoarse, "Thank you! Thank you for carrying My Cross!"[6] Did those who witnessed such personal involvement and identification with the Cross of Christ remember His earlier words, "Anyone who does not carry his cross and follow me cannot be my disciple"?[7] Have you been hiding your identification with Christ because you recoil with repulsion from the shame and suffering of the Cross?

Captain Jeremiah Denton was a prisoner of war in North Vietnam for seven years and seven months, including four years in solitary confinement. America watched with unabashed emotion the day Captain Denton was released and returned to his native America. He arrived home in a plane that taxied up to a strip of bright red carpet, banked by hundreds of microphones, reporters, and photographers. When he stepped off the plane and onto the carpet, we all watched with bated breath, anxious to hear his first words. We didn't have to wait long. With a face deeply etched by suffering, yet with a voice that was clear and strong, the captain said, "We are honored to have had the opportunity to serve our country under difficult circumstances"[8]

On that day, Captain Jeremiah Denton gave us a life's lesson. He expressed humble gratitude for having been able to serve his country, even though that service had involved unspeakable suffering. Could that attitude be what Jesus meant when He said we have to take up our cross and follow Him if we want to be His disciples? And when we arrive in our heavenly home, will we step up and say, "We were honored to serve our King, carrying the Cross of God's will, even when that service included personal suffering"? Carry the Cross. He promises that if you do, you will share in the power of His resurrection and the glory of His crown.[9]

As Jesus struggled to make His way through the narrow streets crowded with the throngs of pilgrims who had come to celebrate the Feast of the Passover, He heard not only cheers and jeers, but also tears. He did not rebuke the mockery, but He did rebuke the misery of a large group of women who wept and wailed for Him. He actually stopped on His way to Calvary and admonished, "Daughters of Jerusalem, do not weep for me; weep for yourselves and for your children" because of the judgment of God that would fall on them because of that day.[10] Jesus flatly rejected their sympathy and pity.

As we meditate on the sacrifice of the Lamb of God, we need to beware of feeling sorry for Him. Instead, our hearts should be crushed from the weight of sorrow for our own sin that cost Him His life—sin that provokes the judgment of God on us unless we confess it and repent of it.

Jesus was not a helpless victim of Roman cruelty or religious jealousy or general apathy. He was the Lamb of God Who was deliberately sacrificed for the sin of the world. Yet He was as human as He was divine, and in His humanity He suffered.

He Suffered Physically

At this point in the Gospel narratives, each writer seems to have turned away. The details are so scant that it gives us the impression the authors could not bear to recall or relate the atrocities they witnessed that day. It's almost as though they drew a protective veil of silence around their beloved Savior, refusing to describe the indescribable. And so we tread reverently and worshipfully on holy ground as we attempt to glimpse something of the price Love paid for you and me.

When Jesus finally arrived at the place of execution around nine o'clock in the morning, if His treatment followed standard procedure in those days, He was stripped of all His clothes.[11] Possibly He was allowed to retain a loincloth. He was then offered, as a humane gesture, a sedative to dull the initial shock and excruciating pain of the spikes being driven through His flesh.[12] However, Jesus refused the offering. Was it because He wanted to "drink the cup the Father had given" Him to the dregs? Did He want to remain fully alert in order to finish the work He had yet to do from the Cross itself—to fulfill prophecy and forgive a dying thief and care for His mother?

Whatever His reasons for refusing the sedative, He was then laid out on the Cross, His arms were outstretched on the horizontal beam at right angles to His body, and nails were driven through His wrists, pinning His hands to the rough wood. His knees were then bent slightly as His feet were placed on a block of wood and spikes were driven through His ankles into the tall center pole. The entire Cross, with Jesus pinned to it by the nails through His wrists and ankles, was then raised upright and dropped into a prepared hole where dirt was tamped around it. Jesus, the Lamb of God, God's own Son, was sacrificed on the altar of a wooden Roman cross.

Normally, crucifixion victims cursed and screamed obscenities and even passed into unconsciousness from the initial pain. Jesus reacted in a stunningly different way—He prayed, "Father, forgive them, for they do not know what they are doing."[13] Fifty days later when Peter preached at Pentecost, Jesus' prayer was answered when some of the very men who crucified Him repented of their sins, placed their faith in Him, and were baptized in His Name![14]

If God could forgive the men who nailed His Son to the Cross, why do you think He won't forgive you? What do you think is beyond the forgiveness of God? Abortion? ~ Adultery? ~ Abuse? ~ Abandonment? ~ Homosexuality? ~ Hate? ~ Hypocrisy? ~ Haughtiness? ~ Doubt? ~ Divorce? ~ Drunkenness? ~ Deception? ~ Murder?~ Or theft? ~ Or immorality? ~ Or_____? You fill in the blank.

It stands to reason that if Jesus asked His Father to forgive the very men who crucified Him, *and God did*, then there is *nothing* and *no one* that He cannot or will not forgive when He is humbly asked.

When have *you* asked?

And if Jesus forgave those who nailed Him to the Cross, and if God forgives you and me, how can you withhold your forgiveness from someone else? How can you withhold your forgiveness from *yourself?* If God says, "I forgive you," who are you to say, "Thank You, God, but I can't forgive myself"? Are your standards higher than His? Are you more righteous than He is? If God says, "I forgive you," then the only appropriate response is to say, "God, thank You. I don't deserve it, but I accept it. And to express my gratitude, I, in turn, forgive that person who has sinned against me."

We forgive others, not because they deserve it, *but because He deserves it!* The only reason we have to forgive is that He commands us to, and our obedience gives us opportunity to say to Him, "Thank You for forgiving me. I love You." Our forgiveness of others then becomes an act of worship that we would not enter into except for Who He is and for the overwhelming debt of love we owe Him.

We will never comprehend what it cost our Lord in physical agony to offer His forgiveness to everyone—no exceptions. But the veil of scriptural silence that shrouds His death in the Gospels is lifted briefly in the Psalms. Psalm 22 gives us an almost eerie insight into how Jesus felt as He hung suspended between heaven and hell, as King David describes a personal experience that was also a prophetic description of Jesus' agony.

The very first words of the psalm are the prayer that was wrenched from our Savior's broken heart and tumbled from His parched lips: "My God, my God, why have you forsaken me? Why are you so far from saving me, so far from the words of my groaning?" *(v. 1)* The pain was so excruciating that He could not remain silent, but groaned and cried out in physical agony. In the midst of intense physical pain, He experienced mental torture, feeling His prayers were getting nowhere, pleading, "O my God, I cry out by day, but you do not answer" *(v. 2)*.

All of our Lord's dignity and self-respect were shattered by the nails, and He felt like "a worm and not a man, scorned by men and despised by the people" *(v. 6)*. Looking down from His vantage point while suffering such extreme physical and mental anguish, He could see His enemies clustered about, staring, gloating, mocking, taunting, insulting, "shaking their heads: 'He trusts in the Lord; let the Lord rescue him. Let him deliver him, since he delights in him'" *(vv. 7–8)*. Yet instead of succumbing to the pressure of pain and lashing out at His Father, He clung by faith to what He knew had been true from the day He was born, when He prayed, "[I] was cast upon you; from my mother's womb you have been my God. Do not be far from me, for trouble is near and there is no one to help" *(vv. 10–11)*.

The psalm continues the prophetic description, noting that as the morning sun rose in the sky and the heat intensified, His open wounds were scorched and the moisture was sucked from His body until He was totally dehydrated and felt "poured out like water." And with the weight of

His body dangling from His wrists, "all my bones are out of joint" *(v. 14)*.

Because of the weight of His body, the only way He could breathe was to push His feet against the block of wood to which they were nailed at a slight angle, raise His body just enough to allow Himself room to gasp for air, then release His weight until once again He hung fully from His wrists. Every movement must have added to His torture, reopening the wounds in His back, tearing at the flesh around the shattered bones in His wrists and ankles, and inflicting even greater pain. But the only way to remain alive was to push up, breathe, then release; push up, breathe, release; push up, breathe, release.[15] Crucifixion was actually a very slow death by suffocation.

The sensation of suffocation would have been over-whelming as His "heart . . . turned to wax; it has melted away within me" *(v. 14)*. After a relatively short period of time, raging fever would have consumed Him until, "My strength is dried up. . . . my tongue sticks to the roof of my mouth; you lay me in the dust of death. Dogs have surrounded me; a band of evil men has encircled me, they have pierced my hands and my feet" *(vv. 15–16)*. His skeleton would have been grotesquely exposed so that "I can count all my bones; people stare and gloat over me. They divide my garments among them and cast lots for my clothing" *(vv. 17–18)*.

Jesus, the Lamb of God, suffered physically as He was sacrificed on the altar of the Cross. In what way are you suffering physically?

Do you have migraine headaches?
Think of the crown of thorns embedded on His brow.

Do you have arthritis?
Think of all His bones pulled out of joint.

Do you have heart disease?
Think of His heart melted like wax within Him.

Do you have cancer?
Think of His raging fever and collapsed lungs.

Many questions about human suffering have no answers.[16] But there is one Answer that transcends all the questions: God, *in the flesh*, knows by personal experience what it *feels like* to suffer physically. Any suffering you or I will ever endure is just a shadow of His, whether physical or emotional.

He Suffered Emotionally

Hymn writers and artists have conveyed to us a picture of Jesus hanging on a Cross on a hill far away. In fact, the place of execution was just outside the city gate, beside the main road leading into Jerusalem. And those to be crucified were only raised two to eighteen inches above the ground. That meant all the dignity and modesty and purity of Jesus' physical person was stripped away and He was left naked to die in searing, scorching heat, writhing and groaning in agony, at virtually eye level with those who passed by on their way to and from the city.

Have you ever had to disrobe so you could be examined by the probing, prying eyes of others? Even if the eyes belong to doctors or nurses or interns or x-ray technicians, the experience can be humiliating. It may have been even worse if you were raped or in some other way physically abused or used. In such circumstances the bitterness of the emotional destruction is much more severe than the physical pain.

Jesus' emotional pain surely increased as people passed Him by. In their rush to get to the temple area in time to purchase a lamb for sacrifice, did the pilgrims preparing for Passover *even notice* the Lamb that God was sacrificing for their sin? As Jesus poured out His life, people must have passed by without a glance, eagerly discussing bargains at the shops, or the weather, or the latest investment opportunities. Have you ever poured out your life for someone who didn't even notice? Jesus understands that kind of emotional pain.

I wonder if others on their way to market were so wrapped up in their grocery lists and errands that they glanced up, read the sign over His head that declared His "crime"—jesus of nazareth, the king of the jews—and clucked their tongues as they commented on the pitiful delusion of the riffraff these days *(John 19:19)*. Perhaps others paused to join in the cruel taunts being hurled at Him: "He saved others, . . . but he can't save himself! He's the King of Israel! Let him come down now from the cross, and we will believe in him. He trusts in God. Let God rescue him now if he wants him, for he said, 'I am the Son of God.'"[17]

At the time of His greatest physical torture, instead of having someone bathe His head with a cold cloth, instead of having someone lovingly sympathize with Him, instead of having any tender care at all, He was mocked and tempted almost beyond human endurance—by those for whom He was dying! That's emotional suffering!

Who is taunting you? Is the taunter someone you have given your life to in marriage? Or in business? Or in school? Or in church? Or in the home?

In what way are you being emotionally tortured? The cruelest of all the taunts hurled at Jesus was surely the one that suggested that if God really loved Him, God would never have allowed Him to be in this situation. Is that how you are being taunted? Is that taunt tempting you to doubt God's love? Is it causing you additional pain? Has someone suggested to you that:

If God really loved you, He would heal your disease?

If God really loved you, He would never have allowed you to lose your job?

If God really loved you, He would bring your spouse back home?

If God really loved you, you would be healthy and wealthy and problem free?

Yet God has said that the proof of His love is none of those things! The proof of His love is that while we were sinners, passing Jesus by on the road of life, He sent His only, beloved Son to die for us.[18]

Even in the blackness of hate and evil swirling around the Cross, the love of God broke through like the rays of the sun on a stormy day. That love shone down on the two thieves crucified on each side of Jesus. Their agony and fury boiled over and spewed out in a venom of curses and taunts hurled at Jesus, challenging Him to save Himself and them.[19]

But one of the thieves grew quieter and quieter, until finally he rebuked his partner in crime, "Don't you fear God . . . since you are under the same sentence? We are punished justly, for we are getting what our deeds deserve. But this man has done nothing wrong." And then, in one of the most moving conversion scenes in human history, the thief turned his face toward Jesus and pleaded in humble faith, "Jesus, remember me when you come into your kingdom." And Jesus turned his face toward the thief and promised, "I tell you the truth, today you will be with me in paradise."[20]

In the twinkling of an eye, that thief changed his eternal destiny; he passed from death to life, had his sins forgiven, and was made right with God. There was no formula or ritual or water baptism or good works, just faith in Jesus.

What do you think you have to do to be saved? Do you think you have to be baptized to be saved?[21] Do you think you have to do something to deserve eternal life? The thief was pinned to a cross! He could barely move his head! He was dying, yet when he placed his faith in Jesus, he was made right with God and granted entrance into His heavenly home! He may have just squeaked through the gates of heaven by the skin of his teeth, but he was in! Do you think it is too late to be forgiven? It's never too late! Because the Lamb makes sin forgivable for everyone, even a dying thief!

Under the scorching sun, with blood dried and caked on His face, with flies and gnats feeding on His broken flesh, with His lips cracked and His throat parched, Jesus surveyed the scene below Him through swollen eyelids. His gaze fell on one of His disciples and a pitiful group of women huddled nearby, their haggard faces showing signs of shock. One of the women was His own mother, Mary.

How could she bear to watch her Son tortured? Yet how could she tear herself away? Did her memory flash back to that night so long ago when her time had come and the only available place for delivery was a stable? Did she remember when she first gazed on His tiny face and traced His curling lashes and rosebud mouth with her finger? Could she still feel the grip of His tiny hand clinging to hers? Did she remember frantically searching for Him in Jerusalem, only to find Him in the temple, already confidently going about His Father's business at the age of twelve? Did she remember the expression in His eyes when He looked at her, and the rich tone of His voice when He spoke to her, and the way He called her name, and . . . was that her Son calling her now?

Mary's entire body must have quivered as though from an electric shock as she heard Jesus calling to her from the Cross. Surely her breath caught as she strained to hear His words, yet He spoke clearly, "'Dear woman, here is your son,' and to the disciple [John], 'Here is your mother.' From that time on, this disciple took her into his home" (John 19:26–27). And somehow, even with the horror of the scene before her reflected in her eyes, and the weight of agony pressing against her chest so that her breathing was labored, she knew everything was going to be all right. She didn't understand, but in the midst of the anguish only a mother knows as her heart is shattered by the pain of her child, a quiet peace must have stolen its way within when God spoke directly and personally to her from the Cross.

God had singled her out, He had noticed her, He had cared for her, and she was comforted.

In His tender, thoughtful care for His mother, Jesus, as He was dying, gives you and me a powerful lesson in how to overcome emotional suffering. Most of us increase our pain by dwelling on it or by analyzing it. We throw a pity party and expect others to join us. We spiral downward into depression, withdrawing into self-preoccupation. But the way to overcome is not to focus on ourselves or on the pain, but to focus on the needs of others.

Would you get your eyes off yourself and your problems and your pressures and your pain and look around? Who do you know who is suffering or struggling in some way? What can you do for them? Ask God to bring to your attention those you can care for. Because as you do, you will find joy in easing their burden, and in the process, you will ease your own. Jesus, at the height of His physical and emotional suffering, looked out for others as He forgave the dying thief and made arrangements for the care of His mother.

Hanging on the Cross, Jesus suffered physical pain and emotional torment that are beyond our comprehension. Yet the spiritual suffering He endured was even worse!

He Suffered Spiritually

In our increasingly secularized society, spiritual suffering is often ignored. It seems to get categorized under all sorts of psychosomatic labels. We may try to drug it, drown it, or lock it up, but it doesn't go away because it is very real. The spiritual suffering of Jesus is not as easily recognizable as His physical and emotional suffering, but it was by far the worst suffering of all. We first glimpse it when Jesus was stripped of His robe and left to hang virtually naked before the world. The emotional shame and humiliation would have been acute for any dignified Jewish rabbi. Yet it wouldn't even have warranted an honorable mention alongside the spiritual humiliation He endured as He was spiritually stripped of His robe of righteousness in God's eyes.

We are first made aware of this type of humiliation in the Garden of Eden when Adam and Eve were naked, yet they seemed to feel no shame or self-consciousness. Some scholars believe they may have been clothed in shimmering light, but that was all. But when they disobeyed God and ate of the fruit He had forbidden, "they realized they were naked; so they sewed fig leaves together and made coverings for themselves . . . and they hid from the Lord God among the trees of the garden."[22] In some way, as soon as they sinned, their physical nakedness was associated with shame and guilt. Their clothing, whatever it had been physically, had also been their spiritual right-relationship with God. When they sinned against Him, they lost that righteousness and in the same poignant scene described in my book, *God's Story*, they stood before each other, dirty in sin and feeling very exposed. They were ashamed of themselves and ashamed of each other, but that didn't begin to compare with their feeling of shame before God. They were so ashamed that just the thought of having to face Him sent them scurrying for a cover-up. The fig leaves they chose to sew together were totally inadequate. God could see right through them.

What fig leaves have you sewn together as a cover-up for your sin and shame before God? Fig leaves . . .

of good works?
of religiosity?
of church attendance?
of community volunteerism?
of morality?
of philanthropy?

There are no fig leaves thick enough or big enough to hide your sin and shame from God.[23]

Unlike Adam and Eve, when Jesus hung on the Cross, He had no fig leaves to use as a covering, inadequate as they were, and He had no bushes to crouch behind. He was totally exposed, not just physically before all people, but also spiritually before God. He didn't just take our sins upon Himself, He *became* those sins for us.[24] Imagine how dirty and vile and evil and guilty and *ashamed* Jesus must have felt as He hung there before a holy God with our sins exposed *as though they were His*!

Jesus' extreme sensitivity to sin can be illustrated by the sensitivity nonsmokers can have to cigarette smoke. For instance, when I check into a hotel room where someone has smoked, even if it was weeks before my arrival, I get a headache. I'm just extremely sensitive to cigarette smoke, a sensitivity that is sharpened by the fact that I've never smoked. If I walk into a room full of smokers, I become nauseated. But my sensitivity to cigarette smoke is just a faint shadow compared to the sensitivity Jesus would have had toward sin and guilt. Jesus had never sinned. Not even once! Can you imagine how exceedingly sensitive He would have been to even the smallest sin? Yet He bore, not just the smallest sins, but all the sins—of all the people—of all the generations—of all the ages—of all the worlds—for all time!

Jesus, in His humanity, knew what the guilt and shame of hatred, of murder, of rape, of stealing, of lying, feels like, as well as every other sin, big or small, that's ever been thought of or committed. As He hung on the Cross, stripped of His own robe of righteousness, He was exposed, spiritually naked in our sins with no hiding place from His Father's penetrating gaze of searing holiness.

Have you ever been caught doing something you shouldn't have? Caught breaking the speed limit? Caught sneaking a piece of cake on your diet? Caught in a lie? Caught in gossip? Do you remember the guilty feeling of shame? That's only a glimmer of the emotional trauma Jesus experienced as He was "caught" in your sins and mine.

Yet because Jesus was stripped "naked," you and I can be clothed! The Bible tells us that all of our righteousness, including the very best things we ever do, are so permeated with sin and selfishness that they are like filthy rags in God's sight.[25] But at the Cross, Jesus gave us His perfect, spotless robe of righteousness and took our filthy garments of sin in exchange.[26] On Judgment Day, you and I will be dressed in His righteousness before God because He wore the filthy garments of our sin.

When Jesus was stripped of His physical clothes, the

execution squad of soldiers divided what little He had between them—His belt, sandals, and other things. But when it came to His beautifully woven inner garment, they decided that instead of tearing it into four pieces, they would gamble for it. So while Jesus hung slightly above them, groaning in excruciating pain, fighting for His breath, they callously ignored Him and tossed the dice *(John 19:23–24)*. Their ribald laughter and the clatter of the dice as they were thrown made a sharp contrast to His pain-wracked sobs so near by.

People today still toss the dice for the robe of His righteousness. While coldly ignoring His death on the Cross, they gamble for His "robe" by betting their eternal lives on the chance that they can earn acceptance with God through their religiosity, or their sincerity, or their morality, or their philanthropy. They "bet" that

if they read their Bibles every day,

if they just do more good works than bad works,

if they keep the Ten Commandments,

if they go to church regularly,

if they're good,

then they have a "chance" to please God and get to heaven—they have a chance to get His "robe." But His "robe" cannot be gambled for, bought, earned, deserved, inherited, given, bartered, or stolen.

The only way to obtain it is to exchange it for your own filthy shreds of righteousness at the Cross. His robe is free, not because it is cheap, but because it is priceless. The guilt of your sin and mine has been removed because it was placed on Him, and His righteousness was placed on us! Praise God! What an exchange!

Jesus hung on the Cross for three hours, wracked with white-hot physical pain, tortured mentally and emotionally by the taunting and the tempting and the trauma, crushed by the weight of guilt and shame and sin that was ours but became His. Suddenly, the birds stopped chirping, the vultures stopped circling, the breeze stopped blowing, and everything became deathly still as darkness—pitch-black darkness—descended. The cries that could be heard were no longer just coming from the victims on the crosses but from the bystanders as they cowered, then fled in panic like rats scurrying to leave a sinking ship. Even the hardened soldiers must have shuddered at the supernatural power and anger that permeated the atmosphere.

As terrified people looked up, searching the sky, there were no clouds to block the sun. There was no eclipse. The sun was nowhere to be seen![27] Where it had been was just blackness! Why? Why was the world plunged into what seemed like the very pit of hell?[28]

The eerie darkness that descended was not just nature feeling sorry for the Creator who was nailed to the altar of the Cross. It was the very judgment of God for your sins and mine that was poured out on Jesus![29] What He went through is beyond our ability to imagine or describe. I do know that because Jesus is God, as well as Man, He may have entered an eternal state of time as He hung on the Cross.

God created time for your benefit and mine—sixty-second minutes and sixty-minute hours and twenty-four-hour days were set in motion by the tides and the rotation of the earth on its axis. But God does not live by our time clocks. He transcends time. That's why Peter said that one day with the Lord is as a thousand years, and a thousand years is as a day.[30] That's why it may be that He created the world in six days on our time clocks, but thousands of years (even millions of years?) on His time clock.[31] Could it be that although Jesus hung on the Cross for six hours according to our time clock, it was actually *an eternity of time on His clock*? Did Jesus live through *an eternity of God's judgment* for your sin and my sin as He hung there on the Cross? We won't know the answer until we get to heaven, but we do know that He took God's judgment for us. He paid the price in full, and He paid for it with His life.

In the Old Testament, Abraham's faith was tested when God told him to take his son, his only son, the son he loved, and offer him as a sacrifice. And Abraham did. Abraham bound Isaac to the altar and raised his knife to slay him in strict obedience to God's Word. Just before the gleaming knife plunged down, God leaned out of heaven and urgently commanded, "Abraham! Abraham! . . . Do not lay a hand on the boy," and Isaac's life was spared! Abraham looked around; caught in the thicket nearby was a ram. After cutting Isaac loose, Abraham took the ram and offered it on the altar. And I wonder, did Isaac embrace the ram with tears streaming down his cheeks, knowing it was a substitute that would die in his place?[32]

As God's Son, God's only Son, the Son He loved, hung on the Cross, the knife of God's fierce wrath against sin was lifted, and there was no one to stay the Father's hand. Instead, "He . . . did not spare his own Son, but gave him up for us all."[33] Jesus was God's Lamb and our Substitute Who endured the full force of God's wrath for your sins and mine when He was bound on the altar in our place.

At midafternoon, the silent darkness was pierced with a heart-wrenching cry that would have sent chills down even the stiffest backs. It came from the cracked lips and the crushed heart of God's Son as His tortured body and fevered mind were pushed to the outer limits of endurance. "My God, my God, why have you forsaken me?"[34] For the first time in eternity, the Father and Son were actually separated.[35] They were separated by all of your sins and my sins, which came between Them. And Jesus, suffocating physically, was smothered spiritually by a blanket of loneliness such as He had never known.

Even when Jesus had been alone in a crowd, or alone on a mountainside, or alone on the lake, or alone in a boat, or alone in a room,

He had never truly been alone! His Father had always been with Him. He and His Father were so close they were One.[36] To be separated was a spiritual death that was worse than a living nightmare. *It was hell!*

No one on this side of hell will ever know the loneliness Jesus endured on the Cross—in your place and mine. When we claim the Lamb as our own sacrifice for sin, we will never be separated from God, because Jesus was. Praise

His dear Name! He is still Emmanuel—God with us. The sacrifice of the Lamb is absolutely sufficient in itself to take away our sin and reconcile us to God.

The Lamb Is Sufficient

The blood of Jesus is sufficient for the forgiveness of any and all sins[37] because the Cross was two thousand years ago and all of our sins were still to come. Therefore, all of our sins, whether we committed them yesterday or today or have yet to commit them tomorrow, are covered by His blood—past sins, present sins, future sins, big sins, small sins, or medium-size sins—it makes no difference.

A few years ago, I found myself groping for a way to explain this to a woman who had been on death row for multiple murders and would be executed within ten hours of my visit. Tears glistened in her eyes as she looked at me beseechingly, needing assurance of the salvation she had claimed by faith six years earlier. That very night she would be stepping into eternity, and she was desperate for reassurance of her forgiveness by God.

I asked her if she had ever been to the ocean, and she nodded yes. I asked her if, as she had walked along the shore, she had seen small holes in the sand where ghost crabs had darted in and out. Again she nodded affirmatively. I then asked if she had seen any larger holes, like those made by children digging a deep moat around a sand castle. Beginning to look somewhat puzzled, she said yes, she had seen holes like that. I persisted as I probed gently to see if she had ever seen huge holes created by machines dredging a channel or burying pipe lines on the beach. Her brow began to furrow as she again acknowledged a quiet yes. I then leaned toward her and pressed my point, "Velma, when the tide comes in, what happens to *all* those holes? The little ones made by the crabs, and the medium-size ones made by children, and the great big ones made by machines?"

A soft light began to gleam in her eyes, and a smile played at the corner of her lips as I answered my own question: "All the holes are covered equally by the water, aren't they? The blood of Jesus is like the tide that washes over the 'holes' of your sins and covers all your sins equally." And Velma stepped into eternity reassured of her forgiveness by God and a welcome into her heavenly home based on *nothing but the blood of Jesus!*

Praise God for the blood of Jesus that is sufficient to cover all of our sins! *All of them!* Big sins like murdering your own mother. Little sins like gossip. Medium-size sins like losing your temper. They are all under the blood of Jesus, and we are free just to enjoy our forgiveness! We will never be held accountable for the guilt of our sins because Jesus has taken the punishment for us.

This lesson was brought home to me when a thunderstorm broke one Wednesday morning, deluging everything and everyone with rain as I arrived at the church to teach my weekly Bible class. In just a few moments, the parking lot became a fast-flowing two-inch-deep river, and the steps to the church looked like a multitiered waterfall. As I stood in the narthex looking through the sheets of wind-swept rain,

I could see a stream of cars organizing itself into neat rows, their headlights sparkling in the raindrops. As I continued to watch, I noticed one woman make a mad dash from her car to the church, umbrella still tightly folded in her hand. She burst through the door, hair askew, makeup smeared, and clothes dripping with water. I sprang to help her, taking her Bible and notebook while she began to shake herself off. I couldn't help but ask with some astonishment, "You have an umbrella. Why didn't you put it up?"

She laughingly replied, "I thought it was just too much trouble."

The rain that fell on everyone and everything that morning is like the wrath of God that falls on all of us because we have all sinned.[38] It is inevitable that sooner or later we will come under His wrath and get "wet." But God has given us an "umbrella" in the blood of Jesus. When we "put it up" by claiming His death for our sins, the umbrella of His blood covers us. God's wrath still falls on our sins, but now our sins are on Jesus; under the umbrella of His blood, we stay dry, and we are saved from the rain of God's wrath.

There is only one umbrella that is sufficient to save us or keep us dry in the midst of the storm of God's wrath. God gave you and me the umbrella when He sent Jesus to the Cross to shed His blood for you. Are you still clutching it tightly, unopened? Why? Do you think it's just too much trouble to confess your sins, to repent, to claim Jesus as your Savior and surrender your life to Him as Lord? *Please! Go to the trouble!* The umbrella of the blood of Jesus is absolutely sufficient to save you from the rain of God's wrath, but you have to deliberately, consciously, personally put it up! *Put it up!*

As Jesus cried out from the Cross, we can hear Him still clinging by faith to Whom He knew His beloved Father to be—My God. Even as the sound left His lips, the darkness lifted and He called out hoarsely, "I am thirsty" *(John 19:28)*. He wasn't asking for a sedative, but something to moisten His swollen tongue and cracked lips. He had something He wanted to say, and He wanted to say it so the angels in heaven would hear it, and the demons in hell would hear it, and people throughout the ages would hear it, and you would hear it, and I would hear it. One of the soldiers standing guard soaked a sponge in wine vinegar, "put the sponge on a stalk of the hyssop plant, and lifted it to Jesus' lips" *(John 19:29)*.

After nine hours of standing on His feet, after being scourged, slapped, and manhandled, after six hours of hanging on the Cross, the average person would have barely had enough life and breath left to even whisper. But Jesus, the Lamb of God, with life still fully flowing through His body, shouted out in a clear, ringing, triumphant voice, "It is finished" *(John 19:30)*.[39] The price for our redemption had been paid! The sacrifice for our sin had been made! Sin was forgiven! Guilt was atoned for! Eternal life was now offered! Heaven has been opened! *It is finished!*

You don't have to do more good works than bad works.
You don't have to go to church every time the door opens.
You don't have to count beads.
You don't have to climb the stairs to some statue.

You don't have to lie on a bed of nails.

You don't have to be religious.

You don't even have to be good!

It is finished! Sin is forgivable for everyone! The price has been paid! *Jesus paid it all!*

Hallelujah!

Hallelujah!

HALLELUJAH!

HALLELUJAH!

As the clarion shout of victory still echoed in the air, Jesus irrevocably handed His life to His Father as He uttered His last words in a ringing declaration of faith: "Father, into your hands I commit my spirit."[40] Then He bowed His head and deliberately refused to take the next breath. He just refused to push up. The One Who is the Lord of life,

the Resurrection and the Life,

the Creator of life,

the Source of all life,

gave His life for you and me!

And the blood of the Lamb that was shed on the altar of the Cross that day ran down the wooden beam, down a hill called Calvary, and down through the years until it reaches us, where it has become a river that is deep enough to bathe in.

—Anne Graham Lotz
Just Give Me Jesus

1. *Hebrews 10:4.*

2. *John 1:29.*

3. *Although this chapter is based primarily on John 19, I have included portions from the other three Gospels in order to convey a more complete picture of these events. Each place where I have drawn from the other Gospels is endnoted for your information.*

4. *Luke 23:33 KJV.*

5. *Luke 23:27; Mark 15:21.*

6. *Simon's brief brush with the blood of Christ changed his life. How could it not? His entire family became involved in the work of the Gospel to the extent that his wife was considered like a mother to the apostle Paul, and his sons Rufus and Alexander became leaders in the early church. See Mark 15:21 and Romans 16:13.*

7. *Luke 14:27.*

8. *The biography of Jeremiah A. Denton Jr., can be found at http://www.nff.org.*

9. *Romans 8:17.*

10. *Luke 23:28.*

11. *Mark 15:24.*

12. *Mark 15:23.*

13. *Luke 23:34.*

14. *Acts 2:36, 38, 41.*

15. *Medical doctors tell us that the strongest instinct we possess is the instinct to breathe. Therefore a crucified victim could not just willfully collapse and refuse to breathe because his instinct took over and forced him to continue pushing up until physical weakness overcame him and he could not. History records that some victims survived as long as nine days on a cross. In this particular case, on Friday evening the guards were told to take down the crucified bodies of Jesus and the thieves on each side of Him so they wouldn't be hanging there on Passover. When the guards checked the bodies, they were amazed that Jesus was already dead. And in order to hasten the death of the two thieves, the guards broke their legs so that they could no longer push up and breathe. See John 19:31–33.*

16. *Some of the unanswerable questions about human suffering are: Why do the innocent suffer? Why do bad things happen to good people? Why does hate seem to triumph over love? Why does evil seem to win out over good? Why do the wicked seem to prosper while the righteous are defeated?*

17. *Matthew 27:41–43.*

18. *Romans 5:8.*

19. *Luke 23:39.*

20. *Luke 23:40–43.*

21. *Water baptism is essentially a symbolic "work" that gives outward testimony to our inward decision to receive Jesus Christ as our Savior. It is necessary for obedience to God's Word, but not for salvation, since the Bible clearly tells us we are saved by faith in Jesus alone. Compare Acts 2:38 with Ephesians 2:8–9.*

22. *Genesis 3:7–8.*

23. *Lotz, God's Story, 76.*

24. *2 Corinthians 5:21.*

25. *Isaiah 64:6.*

26. *2 Corinthians 5:21; Philippians 3:9; 1 Corinthians 1:30; Romans 10:4.*

27. *Luke 23:44–45.*

28. *The Bible describes hell as a place God has prepared for the devil, his angels (or demons), and those who refuse His gracious offer of salvation through faith in Jesus Christ. See Revelation 19:20, 20:10, 15. But we also think of hell, not just as a place, but as a state of eternal separation from God, which is what Jesus experienced at the Cross for us.*

29. *Once before, in Egypt, God's judgment had taken on the form of darkness. See Exodus 10:21–22. And at the end of human history, God's judgment will once again take the form of darkness. See Joel 2:31.*

30. *2 Peter 3:8.*

31. *For a more complete explanation, see Lotz, God's Story, xx–xxii.*

32. *Genesis 22:1–14.*

33. *Romans 8:32.*

34. *Matthew 27:46.*

35. *In a conversation I had with a very godly woman about our Lord's heart-wrenching prayer from the Cross, she emphatically told me she believed Jesus was not forsaken but only felt forsaken. I responded by pointing out to her that Jesus is the Truth. And He did not cease being the Truth when He hung on the Cross. Jesus did not say, "God, I feel so forsaken." He clearly said, "My God, why have You forsaken Me?" Jesus was experiencing the very depths of the pit of hell and judgment as your sins and mine became a barrier between His Father and Himself that caused Them to be truly separated.*

36. *John 10:30.*

37. *1 John 1:7.*

38. *Romans 3:23; Ephesians 2:1–3.*

39. *Matthew 27:50; Mark 15:37.*

40. *Luke 23:46.*

Seizing Hope

Franklin Graham

I want to ask you a pointed question: If you had been in the World Trade Towers that morning of 9/11, would you have been ready for death? Most of us do not dwell on the thought of death. A visit to Ground Zero causes one to give it some thought. Whether God blesses us with a long life or a short life, there is one thing we all have in common—the grave. Eventually, whether in a tragedy like the World Trade Center, from cancer in a hospital bed, or a heart attack in our sleep, we all will face death someday. Do you know your eternal destiny? . . .

Knowledge about God never saved anyone. It is not enough to know the story of Jesus. You must know Him personally.

The Bible makes it very clear that God loves us. He cares for us and He wants us to live our lives to the fullest. But for most people, there is emptiness in their lives that they can't explain. Something is missing. They search for it, through various religions, through relationships, through the acquisition of things money can buy, but that emptiness is still in the pit of their soul. There is a vacuum inside all of us—it can only be filled by God when we come into a right relationship to Him.

We can have a relationship with Him. How? Through His Son, Jesus Christ. He is the mediator between God and man. He is not still hanging on a Roman cross. He is alive in heaven—and He loves you. You can have a new life of meaning and purpose, free from guilt. How does that occur? I want to pose a few simple questions that will clarify the facts concerning the most important decision any person will ever make.

Do you feel that something is missing deep down in your very soul?

Do you feel an emptiness that you cannot explain—sometimes a loneliness—even though you may be in the midst of a crowd?

Most people do. In moments when we are most thoughtful about the meaning of life, there is a craving for something more. At its core, this is a longing to know God intimately. Often people try to fill this emptiness with other things—like alcohol, drugs, food, sexual adventures. The list is long. However, none of these can fill this emptiness, or take away this inner loneliness.

The truth is that God wants to supply what is missing deep inside your soul. He wants to have a relationship with all of us. Each one of us must make a choice to let God into our lives.

We need to understand what it takes to have a right relationship with God; for one day, we will all stand before Him.

What separates you from God? What causes that emptiness in your life?

It is sin.

In today's tolerant culture where "anything goes," many do not understand what sin means. Sin is breaking God's laws. When you disobey God's laws, it separates you from Him.

No matter how hard we try, none of us are able to live life without breaking God's laws. The Bible says: "for all have sinned and fall short of the glory of God,"[1] and "the wages of sin is death."[2] This is the price, this is the penalty . . . this is the sentence. The Supreme Judge—God Himself—has proclaimed that all of mankind is guilty. Everyone has a sin problem. There is no escaping this because God is morally perfect and "holy" and demands that anyone who comes near Him must be holy too.

So how do we as sinners ever solve this dilemma? God's answer comes through the perfect life, death, and resurrection of a substitute sacrifice for our sins—the Lamb of God, His Son—the Lord Jesus Christ. He is the One who paid our debt of sin. We could not possibly pay it.

The Bible tells us, "God so loved the world that He gave His only begotten Son, that whoever believes on Him should not perish but have everlasting life."[3]

And that "whoever" is you and me. Jesus is the only way to God, because He is the only One in history to take sin's penalty for you and me. Buddha did not die for our sins; Muhammad did not die for our sins. No one paid the debt of sin for us except the Lord Jesus Christ—when He shed His blood on Calvary's cross, went to the grave, and rose again on the third day. The only way we can come to God is by faith through His Son and Him alone.

Jesus is the only door we can pass through to meet God the Father.

Do you believe? Are you willing to trust Jesus Christ as your personal Savior? What is your response?

Do not put off making a decision for Christ. The Bible says, "Behold, now is . . . the day of salvation."[4]

"God...desires all men to be saved from their sins and to come to the knowledge of the truth. For there is one God and one Mediator between God and men, the Man Christ Jesus, who gave Himself a ransom for all."[5]

We must all put our faith in Jesus Christ. The Bible says that Christ came into the world to save sinners.[6] Salvation is free to anyone who calls on the Lord Jesus Christ and repents of their sin. It is a gift from God that one can accept. The Bible says," the gift of God is eternal life in Christ Jesus our Lord."[7]

A story was told years ago about a man who was imprisoned for murder. Because he was a model prisoner, the governor decided to offer him a pardon. When the warden came into his cell and told him that the governor had pardoned him and that he was free to go, he refused the pardon. They were bewildered. The case had to go back to the courts to see if the condemned had the right to refuse the governor's pardon. The courts had no choice but to carry out the execution of the condemned man. This is the way it is with us. Because of our sin, we are condemned and sentenced to death; but God offers us a pardon—through receiving His Son, Jesus Christ, by faith. The point is that you have to be willing to accept the pardon.

"How do I do that?" you may ask. "How can I trust this Name above all names, and experience a new and vibrant life, free from guilt and shame?"

It is simple.

First, you must be willing to confess your sins to God, ask Him for forgiveness, and tell Him that you want to change and turn from the sinful life you have been living.

Next, by faith, ask Jesus Christ to come into your life, take control of your life, and to be the Lord of your life.

Then, follow Him from this day forward by obeying Him and reading His instructions found in His Word, the Holy Bible.

If you are willing to do that, God will forgive you and cleanse you. He will give you a new life and a new beginning. As you close this book, you can have that assurance that you have been saved, and that one of these days, when death comes for you, you will have nothing to fear. You will know that for eternity you will be safe in the presence of the King of kings and Lord of lords.

If your desire is to accept Christ as your savior now, just pray this prayer:

> Dear God, I am a sinner. I am sorry for my sins.
> Forgive me. I believe that Jesus Christ is your
> Son. I believe that Jesus Christ died for my sins.
> I want to invite Him into my life. I want to trust
> Him as my Savior and follow Him as my Lord,
> from this day forward, forevermore. In Jesus'
> Name, amen.

If you have prayed that prayer and meant it, I want you to know that God has forgiven you and cleansed you. Your name is now recorded in the Lamb's Book of Life. This is the record of everyone in history who has trusted the Savior. Your name is written there, and it can never be erased.

The Name Above All Names

The brilliant and intense Jewish man—in chains busily writing letter after letter in his Roman jail cell—understood the magnificence of the Name.

The Apostle Paul, in one affectionate note to some old friends in another city, wrote joyfully about why the Name of Jesus reigns above all others:

> And being found in appearance as a man, He humbled Himself and became obedient to the point of death, even the death of the cross. Therefore God also has highly exalted Him and given Him the name which is above every name, that at the name of Jesus every knee should bow, of those in heaven, and of those on earth, and of those under the earth, and that every tongue should confess that Jesus Christ is Lord, to the glory of God the Father.[8]

While our King and Lord waits for the moment when the Father will end human history and authorize Jesus to return —this time not as a humble baby but in the clouds where every eye will see Him[9]—Jesus sits in a place of honor at the right hand of God the Father. He is not idle! Jesus came as a servant, and He is still serving today by interceding on our behalf, at His Father's right hand, through prayer.

> But [Jesus], because He continues forever, has an unchangeable priesthood. Therefore He is also able to save to the uttermost those who come to God through Him, since He always lives to make intercession for them.[10]

Not only is he making intercession for us. He is also preparing us a place. Jesus said:

> Let not your heart be troubled; you believe in God, believe also in Me. In My Father's house are many mansions; if it were not so, I would have told you. I go to prepare a place for you. And if I go and prepare a place for you, I will come again and receive you to Myself; that where I am, there you may be also.[11]

Some day—could it be today?—the trumpet will sound. In Jesus' own words, here's what will happen:

> When the Son of Man comes in His glory, and all the holy angels with Him, then He will sit on the throne of His glory. All the nations will be gathered before Him . . .[12]

Our God is a gracious and patient Father, but when He lowers the curtain on mankind's story, the play will be over.

As Paul wrote in that letter to his friends at Philippi, every knee will bow and every tongue will confess, "Jesus Christ is Lord."

All knees will bow and every tongue will confess, including·

Abraham, the pharaohs, Moses,
    Mary and Joseph, the disciples
John the Baptist, the Pharisees, Herod, Pilate,
    the Apostle Paul
Roman emperors, Alexander the Great, Constantine
Winners and losers
Columbus, Cortés, Perry, Lindberg, Armstrong
Popes, Muhammad, Mahatma Gandhi,
    Mother Teresa
Washington, Lincoln, Roosevelt, Kennedy, Reagan
Kings, queens, princes, and princesses
George Wishart, Cassie Bernall, and all
    martyrs wearing their white robes
Babe Ruth, Tiger Woods, Joe Montana,
    America's Cup winners
Mark McGwire, Muhammad Ali
Abortionists and anti-abortionists
Stalin, Hitler, Lenin, Mao, Pol Pot, Bin Laden
Members of the nearly ten thousand religions
Construction workers and doctors
Frank Sinatra, Cher, Michael Jackson, Madonna
Marilyn Monroe, Jimmy Stewart, Mel Gibson,
    Julia Roberts
Martin Luther and Martin Luther King
Millionaires and misfits
Carnegie, Vanderbilt, Rockefeller, Walton, Gates
Moonshiners, mafia, drug lords, pushers, and addicts
Bunyan, Shakespeare, Hemingway,
    Lewis, Grisham
Pornographers, prostitutes, philanthropists,
    and pedophiles

Larry King, Barbara Walters, David Letterman,
    Tom Brokaw
Patriots and terrorists
Van Gogh, Michelangelo, Picasso, Rockwell
Saddam Hussein, Yasir Arafat
Golda Meir, David Ben Gurion, Ariel Sharon
Rachel the Israeli victim and Ayat
    the suicide bomber
Lawyers and longshoremen
Mozart, Beethoven, Gershwin, Lennon
Skeptics and mockers
Voltaire, Freud, Darwin, Madeline Murray
O'Hare
Billy and Ruth Graham
Franklin Graham
Your boss and your neighbor
Your spouse and your child
You

Every knee will bow and every tongue will confess,
"Jesus Christ is Lord." . . .

And then those from every generation, who have
believed in the Name and accepted the gift of eternal life,
will together worship the King:

And they sang a new song . . .
    "For You were slain, . . .
    And have redeemed us to God by Your blood

    Out of every tribe and tongue and people
    and nation . . .
    And we shall reign on the earth."

And every creature which is in heaven and on the
earth and under the earth and such as are in the
sea, and all that are in them, I heard saying:
"Blessing and honor and glory and power
Be to Him who sits on the throne,
And to the Lamb, forever and ever!"[13]

One day we will all stand before Jesus, either as our Savior
or our Judge. I don't know about you, but I am ready to face
the One who is owed all the glory and honor, the One who
bears the Name—JESUS.

—Franklin Graham
The Name

1. Romans 3:23 *NKJV.*

2. Romans 6:23 *NKJV.*

3. John 3:16 *NKJV.*

4. 2 Corinthians 6:2 *NKJV.*

5. 1 Timothy 2:3–6 *NKJV.*

6. See 1 Timothy 1:15.

7. Romans 6:23 *NKJV.*

8. Philippians 2:8–11 *NKJV.*

9. See Revelation 1:7.

10. Hebrews 7:24–25 *NKJV.*

11. John 14:1–3 *NKJV.*

12. Matthew 25:31–32 *NKJV.*

13. Revelation 5:9–10, 13 *NKJV.*

Acknowledgments

BILLY GRAHAM, *Peace with God*, 1953, 1984, W Publishing Group, Nashville, Tennessee. All rights reserved.

FRANKLIN GRAHAM, excerpted by permission of Thomas Nelson Publishers from the book entitled *The Name*, ©2002 by Franklin Graham.

JACK HAYFORD, excerpted by permission of Thomas Nelson Publishers from the book entitled *How to Live Through a Bad Day*, ©2001 by Jack Hayford.

ANNE GRAHAM LOTZ, *Just Give Me Jesus*, 2000, W Publishing Group, Nashville, Tennessee. All rights reserved.

MAX LUCADO, *A Gentle Thunder*, 1995, W Publishing Group, Nashville, Tennessee. All rights reserved.

JOHN MACARTHUR, *The Murder of Jesus*, 2000, W Publishing Group, Nashville, Tennessee. All rights reserved.

CHARLES STANLEY, excerpted by permission of Thomas Nelson Publishers from the book entitled *A Gift of Love*, ©2001 by Charles Stanley.

CHARLES SWINDOLL, *The Darkness and the Dawn*, 2001, W Publishing Group, Nashville, Tennessee. All rights reserved.

| **FAMILY** CHRISTIAN STORES | Coupon Valid 3/1-4/15/03 |

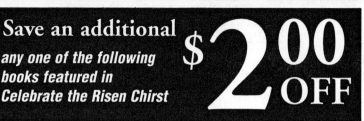

Save an additional

any one of the following books featured in Celebrate the Risen Chirst

$ **2** 00 OFF

BILLY GRAHAM
Peace With God

FRANKLIN GRAHAM
The Name

JACK HAYFORD
How to Live Through a Bad Day

ANNE GRAHAM LOTZ
Just Give Me Jesus

MAX LUCADO
A Gentle Thunder

JOHN MACARTHUR
The Murder of Jesus

CHARLES STANLEY
A Gift of Love

CHARLES SWINDOLL
The Darkness and the Dawn

| **FAMILY** CHRISTIAN STORES | Coupon Valid 4/17-7/31/03 |

Save an additional

any one of the following books featured in Celebrate the Risen Chirst

$ **2** 00 OFF

BILLY GRAHAM
Peace With God

FRANKLIN GRAHAM
The Name

JACK HAYFORD
How to Live Through a Bad Day

ANNE GRAHAM LOTZ
Just Give Me Jesus

MAX LUCADO
A Gentle Thunder

JOHN MACARTHUR
The Murder of Jesus

CHARLES STANLEY
A Gift of Love

CHARLES SWINDOLL
The Darkness and the Dawn

FamILY
CHRISTIAN STORES
Helping to Strengthen Hearts, Minds & Souls

940776

Sales associate key as FBS NON-FLYER COUPON (%)

Cannot be combined with other coupons or Perks Shopping Sprees.
No price adjustments on merchandise previously purchased.
Available in stores on in-stock items only—not applicable on internet or phone orders.

FamILY
CHRISTIAN STORES
Helping to Strengthen Hearts, Minds & Souls

940778

Sales associate key as FBS NON-FLYER COUPON (%)

Cannot be combined with other coupons or Perks Shopping Sprees.
No price adjustments on merchandise previously purchased.
Available in stores on in-stock items only—not applicable on internet or phone orders.

Family
CHRISTIAN STORES

945755

Sales associate key as FBS NON-FLYER COUPON (%)
Cannot be combined with other coupons or Perks Shopping Sprees. Not to be used toward the purchase of gift certificates, VBS, electronics, church and home school curriculum, textbooks or church supplies. No price adjustments on merchandise previously purchased. Available in stores on in-stock items only—not applicable on internet or phone orders.

Family
CHRISTIAN STORES

945756

Sales associate key as FBS NON-FLYER COUPON ($)
Cannot be combined with other coupons or Perks Shopping Sprees. Not to be used toward the purchase of gift certificates, VBS, electronics, church and home school curriculum, textbooks or church supplies. No price adjustments on merchandise previously purchased. Available in stores on in-stock items only—not applicable on internet or phone orders.

Family
CHRISTIAN STORES

945758

Sales associate key as FBS NON-FLYER COUPON (%)
Cannot be combined with other coupons or Perks Shopping Sprees. Not to be used toward the purchase of gift certificates, VBS, electronics, church and home school curriculum, textbooks or church supplies. No price adjustments on merchandise previously purchased. Available in stores on in-stock items only—not applicable on internet or phone orders.

Family
CHRISTIAN STORES

945759

Sales associate key as FBS NON-FLYER COUPON (%)
Cannot be combined with other coupons or Perks Shopping Sprees. Not to be used toward the purchase of gift certificates, VBS, electronics, church and home school curriculum, textbooks or church supplies. No price adjustments on merchandise previously purchased. Available in stores on in-stock items only—not applicable on internet or phone orders.

FAMILY
CHRISTIAN STORES

945760

Sales associate key as FBS NON-FLYER COUPON (%)
Cannot be combined with other coupons or Perks Shopping Sprees. Not to be used toward
the purchase of gift certificates, VBS, electronics, church and home school curriculum,
textbooks or church supplies. No price adjustments on merchandise previously purchased.
Available in stores on in-stock items only–not applicable on internet or phone orders.

FAMILY
CHRISTIAN STORES

945761

Sales associate key as FBS NON-FLYER COUPON (%)
Cannot be combined with other coupons or Perks Shopping Sprees. Not to be used toward
the purchase of gift certificates, VBS, electronics, church and home school curriculum,
textbooks or church supplies. No price adjustments on merchandise previously purchased.
Available in stores on in-stock items only–not applicable on internet or phone orders.

FAMILY
CHRISTIAN STORES

945762

Sales associate key as FBS NON-FLYER COUPON (%)
Cannot be combined with other coupons or Perks Shopping Sprees. Not to be used toward
the purchase of gift certificates, VBS, electronics, church and home school curriculum,
textbooks or church supplies. No price adjustments on merchandise previously purchased.
Available in stores on in-stock items only–not applicable on internet or phone orders.

FAMILY
CHRISTIAN STORES

945763

Sales associate key as FBS NON-FLYER COUPON (%)
Cannot be combined with other coupons or Perks Shopping Sprees. Not to be used toward
the purchase of gift certificates, VBS, electronics, church and home school curriculum,
textbooks or church supplies. No price adjustments on merchandise previously purchased.
Available in stores on in-stock items only–not applicable on internet or phone orders.